AQA Psychology A

AS

Psychology

Research Methods Workbook

Julia Willerton

Nick Lund

Nelson Thornes

Published in 2011 by:
Nelson Thornes Ltd
Delta Place
27 Bath Road
CHELTENHAM
GL53 7TH
United Kingdom

11 12 13 14 15 / 10 9 8 7 6 5 4 3 2 1

A catalogue record for this book is available from the British Library

ISBN 978 1 4085 0817 6

Cover photograph: iStockphoto

Page make-up by Pantek Arts Ltd, Maidstone

Printed and bound in Spain by GraphyCems

Acknowledgements
Page 62, The Negative Event Scale used with kind permission of Dr Daryl Maybery at www.quantifyingconnections.com; page 65, the Locus of Control questionnaire reproduced with the kind permission of Dr Julian Rotter.

Contents

Unit 1 Cognitive Psychology, Developmental Psychology and Research Methods

Unit 2 Biological Psychology, Social Psychology and Individual Differences

This workbook is designed to help you broaden your understanding of psychological research by carrying out actual psychological research yourself. You will also develop your critical understanding by thinking and talking with your teachers and fellow students. Discuss what worked well – but remember that you can learn as much, if not more, when things do not go as planned. Carrying out practical work will also help you to write more effectively when answering exam questions about the strengths and weaknesses of particular research methods.

Each of these research projects relates to a topic area from the Psychology AS course. These exercises will help you to understand a range of research methods and tackle the research methods questions in the PSYA1 and 2 exams. The best way to truly understand research methods is to put them to use in practical work.

Each research project includes:

Learning outcomes

The learning outcomes for all of the practicals are listed below. Check the start of each practical to see which learning outcomes it covers.

Methods and techniques

A1 Understand advantages and disadvantages of self-report methods, including surveys and interviews

A2 Understand correlational research

A3 Understand how data can be gathered via interview

A4 Understand the difference between open and closed questions

A5 Understand controlled observation

A6 Collect and record data

Investigation design

B1   Construct or adapt a questionnaire

B2   Design standardised instructions

B3   Design a structured observation data collection sheet

B4   Understand how to ask for consent and debrief participants afterwards

B5   Understand the importance of standardised instructions

B6   Consider the importance of reliability

B7   Operationalise variables

B8   Practise writing experimental hypotheses

B9   Understand how to control extraneous variables

B10 Understand how to select samples

Data analysis and presentation

C1   Understand what is meant by qualitative data
C2   Display data using appropriate graphs and tables
C3   Analyse data using descriptive statistics
C4   Convert qualitative data to quantitative format using content analysis
C5   Report your results in the accepted form
C6   Summarise qualitative data
C7   Summarise quantitative data from a questionnaire using descriptive statistics, tables and graphs

Background

There is a brief summary of the theoretical background to the topic. The Key study is a quick reminder of a related study.

Method

Each practical includes step-by-step instructions to carry out the research.

Think about

These features highlight particular aspects that are important to consider when carrying out research or answering questions on research methods in your exam.

Critical discussion

This includes some of the more important points that you may want to consider and discuss after you have collected and analysed your data.

Glossary and Appendix

Terms relating to research methods can be found in the glossary, and the Appendix contains key documents, including statistical tables.

Ethical issues

Carrying out these research projects will help you to develop your understanding of research within an ethical framework. Ethical issues are raised throughout, but this does not mean that all of the ethical issues have been thought out for you. Whenever you carry out research involving feeling, thinking beings, including both human and non-human animals, you need to be aware of possible ethical issues at all stages of the research process. For this reason, the BPS ethical guidelines are included in the Appendix.

Cognitive psychology

1 Serial position curve – class practical

Learning outcomes for this practical

- A6, B4, B5, B8, B9, C2, C3, C5

Hint

Check these learning outcomes against the list on pages iv–v.

Class practical

Before working through this chapter you should already have been a participant in the experiment described. This allows you to experience an experiment from the point of view of a participant before you carry out your own research. You can also look back at how the experiment was carried out and consider why this way of doing it (the method) was chosen.

If you have not taken part in a free recall experiment, please do not read the rest of the chapter yet. Knowing the full details of the study may alter your responses.

Background

One of the central features of the multi-store model of memory put forward by Atkinson and Shiffrin (1968) was the distinction between short-term memory (STM) and long-term memory (LTM). They suggested that the two memory stores differ in a number of ways. The first is duration. Information is only stored in STM for a matter of seconds, but it can last a lifetime in LTM. The second difference is capacity. A very limited amount of information can be stored in STM (about seven items), but the capacity of LTM seems to be unlimited. A third difference is in the way that the information is stored (or the way it is encoded). STM seems to store information mainly by using acoustic coding, whereas LTM seems to use semantic coding. Finally, the stores differ in the way that information is lost (forgotten).

There is evidence for each of these differences, which does seem to suggest that there is a distinction between the two stores.

One technique used to illustrate the distinction is the free recall task. In this, a group of participants is given a long list of unrelated words to remember and then asked to recall as many as they can in any order. The researcher does not record each individual's total score but rather is interested in how many participants recall each word in the list and, more importantly, where the words appear in the list (the start, middle or end). When plotted on a graph of word position against frequency recalled, this produces a serial position curve.

Typically, words at the end of the list are recalled best followed by words at the beginning. Words in the middle of the list have the lowest recall rate.

Look it up ...

Look in the AS Student Book or elsewhere at some of the evidence (e.g. studies) that STM and LTM are different stores.

It is assumed that the words at the end of the list are recalled because they are still in the STM. This is known as the recency effect. It is thought that the words at the beginning of the list are recalled because they are in the LTM. This is the primacy effect.

This practical exercise investigates the serial position curve. The basic free recall procedure hints at the distinction between STM and LTM but does not really prove it. Glanzer and Cunitz (1966) carried out variations of the basic procedure and they provide such evidence.

Key study

Two storage mechanisms in free recall, Glanzer and Cunitz (1966)

In one variation of the basic free recall experiment, the participants were put into one of two conditions. In the control condition participants were asked to recall the list of words immediately after it was presented. However, in the experimental condition participants were given a distracter task after the list was presented. They were asked to count backwards in threes for 30 seconds. This task causes information in STM to be lost. They found the normal recency effect in the control condition, but there was very little evidence of a recency effect in the experimental condition. This suggests that the lack of a recency effect seen in the experimental condition was due to STM being disrupted by the delay in recall.

In a later experiment, Glanzer and Cunitz investigated the primacy effect. One explanation of why the first few words were recalled well was that they had been rehearsed and therefore stored in LTM. Glanzer and Cunitz investigated this by varying the speed that the words were presented, arguing that if they were presented slowly there was more time for rehearsal. They found that when the words were presented slowly there was a large primacy effect, meaning lots of words towards the beginning of the list were remembered. When there was no gap between words when they were presented, and therefore no opportunity to rehearse information, the primacy effect almost disappeared.

Method

Step 1 *The design of the study: variables and hypotheses*

The first step of the research process is to identify a topic of interest and to choose a suitable method to investigate it. In the class practical, you investigated the recall of words in different positions in a list. The method used was an experiment.

In an experiment, the researcher manipulates an independent variable and measures its effects, if any, on a dependent variable. The experiment that you have just done was unusual because it did not compare the performance of two groups of participants, nor was it a straightforward comparison of the performance of each individual in different conditions. The effect of word position on recall was being investigated. Write down what the independent variable and dependent variable were in this experiment.

Independent variable: _____

Dependent variable: _____

There are a number of experimental designs. The two most common are the independent group and repeated measures designs. To understand which was used in the experiment that you did, you have to consider what was being compared. If you are comparing the results of two different groups of people, the method is an independent group design. If you are comparing the results of one group of people in different conditions, the design is a repeated measure design.

The design used in this study was:

_____

Write a suitable hypothesis (the predictive statement being tested) for the study you have just done. The experimental hypothesis predicts a difference between the conditions. Your experimental hypothesis should be directional as the previous research will have given you an idea about which way it will go.

Fill in the blanks in the hypothesis here.

Words presented at the start and _____ *of the list will*

be recalled _____ *than the words* _____

of the list.

Step 2   *The ethical issues of the study*

Ethical issues guide practical choices and decisions at all stages of the research process. **Think about the ethical issues involved in this piece of research.**

■ An important principle of research is to enable participants to give their fully informed consent to take part, knowing what they will be letting themselves in for. You should have been given an information sheet that told you what was involved in the study, what you would be asked to do and roughly how long it would take. There should also have been a consent form to sign. The consent form should have made it clear that you were free to withdraw at any time.

■ At the end of the study, debriefing information should have been given (usually in written form with verbal support). This should have explained what the experiment was about and the findings that were expected, and it should have asked whether you had any questions.

Step 3 *The sample used in the study*

You are required to know about three types of sample:

- a random sample
- an opportunity sample
- a self-selected (volunteer) sample.

In this study, you and your class were the participants. You were all asked to participate because you were in the class.

Which sample method does this represent?

_____

Step 4 *The stimulus materials and data sheets used in the study*

Review the materials used in the study. Firstly, look at the information sheet and consent form. Does the information sheet give a good description of what you would do as a participant in this study?

The standard instructions for the experiment should be clear and describe exactly what you do. Having done the study, are there any changes that you would make to improve the study or the instructions? If so, these may be worth mentioning in the methodology section of the critical discussion at the end.

The debriefing sheet should give further information about the study and what it expected to find.

Analysing your data

Step 5 *Displaying your data in tables and graphs*

The data for this study are how many participants recalled each word in the list. The scores of individual participants are irrelevant for what is being investigated. You should have a data sheet that shows how many participants recalled word 1, 2, and so on. You should plot these data with the word position from 1 to 20 along the bottom (*x*-axis) so that it looks like the graph opposite.

Look it up …

Remind yourself about the advantages and disadvantages of each of these sampling methods by looking in your AS Student Book or elsewhere.

Think about controls

What other factors, other than word position, might influence recall of individual words? Why was it important to have 20 words that were similar?

Look at the list of words you were asked to remember. You should notice similarities between the words. All of the words are five letters long. They are all fairly common, everyday words.

Ethical issues

If the scores of individuals were important to what was being investigated, then they should have been used anonymously in case they caused distress (in the form of embarrassment) to any individuals.

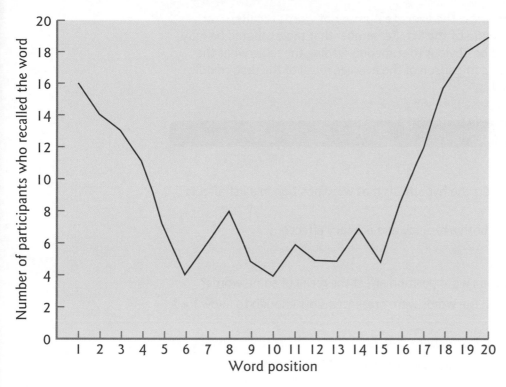

Graph showing frequency of words recalled and their serial position in the list

Step 6 *Descriptive analysis of your results*

Past research suggests that more words should be recalled at the beginning and end of the list than in the middle. In the serial position graph (see Step 5), you can see whether this is true of your results. You could also use some quantitative data to test your hypothesis. One way of doing this is to create three sets of data by taking the totals for the first four words, the last four words and the middle four words. These are three sets of scores that you can compare directly.

You can also contrast the sets of scores much more easily by comparing some measure of central tendency (or averages). There are three measures of central tendency:

- mode
- median
- mean.

Look it up ...

You might want to remind yourself about the advantages and disadvantages of each of the measures of central tendency.

Which is the appropriate measure to use for these results?

_____

Calculate the average for each of the three sets of figures representing the beginning, middle and end of the list.

Draw up a simple table to show the average number of words recalled from the beginning, end and middle of the list. Remember that tables should be fully labelled and clear. It should be obvious to someone reading the table what the results are. This allows easy comparison of the average recall of the first, middle and last four words on the list.

Critical discussion

Theory
- Did your findings support the hypothesis that word position in a list affects recall?
- Was there evidence of both a recency and primacy effect?

Methodology
- Did any factor other than word position affect the recall of some words?
- Was the speed at which the words were presented slow enough to allow for a primacy effect?
- Were your standardised instructions clear?
- Can you suggest any other ways the practical could be improved?

Ethics
- Did your study throw up any unseen ethical issues?
- How did you feel about taking part?
- What have you learned about research with people?

References

Atkinson, R.C. and Shiffrin, R.M. (1968) Human Memory: A proposed system and its control processes. In K.W. Spence and J.T. Spence (eds), *The Psychology of Learning and Motivation* (Vol. 2). London: Academic Press.

Glanzer, M. and Cunitz, A.R. (1966) Two storage mechanisms in free recall. *Journal of Verbal Learning and Verbal Behaviour*, **5**, 351–60.

Cognitive psychology

2 Eyewitness testimony – class practical

> **Learning outcomes for this practical**
> - A6, B4, B5, B8, B9, C2, C3, C5

Hint

Check these learning outcomes against the list on pages iv–v.

Class practical

Before working through this chapter, you should already have been a participant in the experiment described. This allows you to experience an experiment from the point of view of a participant before you carry out your own research. You can also look back at how the experiment was carried out and consider why this way of doing it (i.e. the method) was chosen.

If you have not taken part in an eyewitness experiment, please do not read the rest of the chapter yet. Knowing the full details of the study may alter your responses.

Background

One of the most important applications of memory research is in the study of eyewitness testimony. Eyewitnesses are asked about their memory of an event and these memories are a vital form of evidence. Juries and police officers hold eyewitness testimony in high regard and believe it is good, reliable evidence. However, there is a great deal of evidence that shows this confidence is misplaced. For example, a number of people convicted because of eyewitness testimony have been cleared by more reliable DNA evidence. Some estimates suggest that thousands of people each year may be wrongly convicted by eyewitness evidence. Over the past 40 years, a number of psychologists have produced experimental evidence to show that the memories of eyewitnesses are not accurate.

One of the prominent researchers of eyewitness testimony, Loftus, has demonstrated that eyewitness memories are prone to distortions and reconstruction. For example, when participants are asked leading questions after viewing a film of a car accident it can alter their testimony. If asked: 'Did you see *the* broken headlight?' they are more likely to say yes than if asked: 'Did you see *a* broken headlight?' In other studies Loftus found that post-event information, such as the way that questions were asked, affected later memory of films. Later work has revealed that a variety of other factors also affect eyewitness testimony including expectancy, anxiety and age of the witness. This practical exercise investigates the effect of delay on eyewitness memory.

Look it up ...

Look at your AS Student Book or other resources to review the work on the various factors that affect eyewitness testimony.

Key study

Reconstruction of automobile destruction, Loftus and Palmer (1974)

The Loftus and Palmer study consists of two experiments. In the first, participants were shown film clips and then asked a number questions about them. The crucial question was: 'About how fast were the cars going when they hit each other?' There were five conditions and in each a different verb was used. The verbs were: hit, smashed, collided, bumped and contacted. The estimates of speed varied from an average of 31.8 mph for the verb 'contacted' to 40.8 mph for the verb 'smashed'.

In the second study, the participants were again shown clips and asked questions about what they had seen. One of the questions was about speed. Some participants were asked: 'How fast were the cars going when they hit each other?' and others were asked: 'How fast were the cars going when they smashed each other?' One week later, the same participants were asked another series of questions about the clips. The critical question this time was: 'Did you see any broken glass?' (there was none in the clip). Sixteen of the 'smashed' group said yes compared to only seven of the 'hit' group. This suggests that over time, memories become reconstructed and distorted by other information.

Method

Step 1 *The design of the study: variables and hypotheses*

The first step of the research process is to **identify a topic of interest and choose a suitable method to investigate it**. In the class practical the method used was a field experiment. The same event was seen by all, but one group was asked to recall the event immediately and another was asked to recall it some time later.

In an experiment, the researcher manipulates an independent variable and measures its effects, if any, on a dependent variable. Write down what the independent variable and the dependent variable in this experiment were.

> *Independent variable:* _____
>
> *Dependent variable:* _____

> **Hint**
>
> The study is investigating whether details being recalled might *depend on* whether there was a delay in recalling them or whether details were recalled immediately afterwards.

There are a number of experimental designs. The two most common are the independent measures or groups and the repeated measures designs. Which was used in this study? To understand this it is useful to consider what is being compared. If you are comparing the results of two different groups of people, the method is an independent group design. If you are comparing the results of one group of people in two different conditions, the design is a repeated measure design.

The design used in this study was:

_____

Think about controls

What particular extraneous variables need to be addressed when these two different designs are used?

Write a suitable hypothesis for the study you have just done. You will need to decide whether your experimental hypothesis should be directional or non-directional. Directional hypotheses are chosen when there is sufficient research to point to the outcome of the study. When research has produced conflicting results (i.e. you do not have an idea of the likely effect of the independent variable) then a non-directional hypothesis is appropriate.

Write your hypotheses here.

_____

_____

_____

Justify your choice of a directional or non-directional hypothesis here.

I have chosen a _____ *hypothesis because*

_____

_____

Step 2 *The ethical issues of the study*

Ethical issues guide practical choices and decisions at all stages of the research process. Think about the ethical issues involved in this piece of research.

- An important principle of research is to enable participants to give their fully informed consent to take part, knowing what they will be letting themselves in for. You should have been given an information sheet that told you what was involved in the study, what you would be asked to do and roughly how long it would take. There should also have been a consent form to sign. The consent form should have made it clear that you are free to withdraw at any time.

- At the end of the study, debriefing information should have been given (usually in written form with verbal support). This should have explained what the experiment was about and the findings that were expected, and it should have asked whether you had any questions.

Step 3 *The sample used in the study*

You are required to know about three types of sample:

- a random sample
- an opportunity sample
- a self-selected (volunteer) sample.

In this study, you and your class were the participants. You were all asked to participate because you were in the class.

Which sample method does this represent?

_____

Step 4 *The stimulus materials and data sheets used in the study*

Review the materials used in the study. Look at the information sheet and consent form. Does the information sheet give a good description of what you would do as a participant in this study? The debriefing sheet should give further information about the study and what it expected to find.

The standard instructions for the experiment should be clear and describe exactly what you should do. Having done the study, are there any changes that you would make to improve it? If so, these may be worth mentioning in the methodology section of the critical discussion.

Analysing your data

Step 5 *Descriptive analysis of your results*

You should have two sets of scores: the number of correct items recalled by individuals in the immediate recall group and the number of correct items recalled by individuals in the delayed recall group. It is difficult to understand this mass of raw data and to see any pattern of results that have emerged from the study. You can contrast the two sets of scores much more easily by comparing some measure of central tendency. There are three measures of central tendency:

■ mode
■ median
■ mean.

Which is the most appropriate measure to use for these results?

_____

Explain why this measure is the most appropriate.

_____

_____

Step 6 *Displaying your data in tables and graphs*

Draw a table to show the average number of correct answers from the immediate and delayed recall groups. Remember that tables should be fully labelled and clear. It should be obvious to someone reading the table what your results were.

Ethical issues

Why is debriefing important after asking participants to witness an event on-screen? What sort of emotional state should participants be in when they leave a study?

Think about controls

Control is an important principle of research design. You need to ensure that stimulus materials and instructions are standardised as far as possible.

Look it up ...

Remind yourself about the advantages and disadvantages of each of the measures of central tendency. Look at your AS Student Book or another resource.

Another way of showing patterns of data is to use graphs. As graphs are visual representations of the patterns in data, they should be easy to understand and, for many people, easier to recall when they read the conclusion and discussion. There are many types of graphs including:

- histograms
- bar charts
- scattergrams.

Which type of graph is appropriate to show the difference between the two groups of participants?

_____

Use the data to **draw an appropriate graph**.

> **Think about validity**
>
> Was your study representative of the events that might happen to a real eyewitness?
>
> Make a list of the possible differences between you and a real eyewitness.
>
> Include these in your discussion.

Critical discussion

Theory
- Did the findings support the hypothesis?
- If your experimental hypothesis was not supported, can you think of reasons why this might be?

Methodology
- Did everyone have a clear view of the event that they were supposed to recall?
- Do you think the delay for the delayed recall group was long enough for memory distortion and reconstruction to occur?
- Can you suggest any ways the experiment could be improved?
- Is there a better way to study eyewitness recall?
- Were the standardised instructions clear?

Ethics
- Did the study throw up any unseen ethical issues?
- How did you feel about taking part in the study?
- What have you learned about research with people?

References

Loftus, E.F. and Palmer, J.C. (1974) Reconstruction of automobile destruction: An example of the interaction between language and memory. *Journal of Verbal Learning and Verbal Behaviour*, **13**, 585–9.

Developmental psychology

3 Choosing day care

Learning outcomes for this practical

- A1, A4, A6, B1, B2, B4, B5, C1, C2, C5, C6, C7

Hint

Check these learning outcomes against the list on pages iv–v.

Hint

This practical will work best if you design the questionnaire as a group activity and collect the data from your own psychology classmates and their parents/carers.

Student practical

In this practical you will investigate decisions about the types of day care that parents or carers choose for their children. You will pool the results from the questionnaire to try to answer some specific research questions and display this descriptive data.

Background

Day care is care for young children of preschool age during the daytime. It is often used to enable parents to work, although non-working parents may also use day care to prepare their child for starting school. There are broadly two different kinds of day care available in the UK:

- Family-based care – the child is looked after within a family setting at a childminder's house or in their own home by a relative.

- Nursery-based care – the child attends a day-care centre or nursery school, which can be state or privately run. The child is looked after by trained nursery workers.

These two settings differ in terms of the number of children that are looked after by each adult and the amount of attention each child receives. Children are likely to receive more adult attention in family-care settings and less adult attention at a nursery. In contrast, children who attend nursery will have more opportunities to play with other children, interact and develop social skills than those in family-based care. Some children experience different types of day care for different periods of time, for example starting with a childminder and moving on to nursery.

Key study

Day care, Melhuish (1990)

Melhuish (1990) compared three groups of children in London who started day care before they were nine months old. These children were looked after either by relatives, a childminder or in a private nursery. Melhuish assessed the children at 18 months and 3 years for their language skills and their abilities to cooperate and share with other children.

At 18 months, the babies who had been cared for by relatives had the best-developed language skills. This probably reflects the fact that they would be more likely to have one-to-one attention and would be talked to for a large proportion of the time. In contrast, language skills were least developed in the children who had attended nursery and who would have had less adult attention but more child interaction.

At three years old, the nursery school children showed higher levels of cooperation and sharing than either of the family-based care groups. This probably reflects the fact that they would have had more opportunities to learn and practise these skills in a nursery environment.

Melhuish's study looks at the effects of day care on different aspects of social and cognitive development. However, it also points to the different choices that parents make regarding day care. What factors influence parents' choices about day care? One may be the needs of the child: children vary in terms of attachment styles and temperament. Some are more confident and others are shy and timid. Parents may choose a day-care setting for their child in light of the child's personality (e.g. nursery to bring out a shy child) or the family situation. Another factor influencing choice of day care may be practical issues such as the availability and cost of different types of care in the area. In this practical exercise, you are going to examine the types of day care attended by students in your own Psychology AS group. You should specifically **consider two research questions**:

- What types of day care did students attend and for how long?
- What factors influenced the choices that the parents/carers made about day care?

Research questions are different to hypotheses as they do not look for differences or associations between variables.

Method

Step 1 *The design of the study*

The first step of the research process is to **choose a suitable method to investigate the topic**. There are a number of different ways of investigating use of day care:

- Each student in your group could write down their memories (recollections) of day care.
- Each student could carry out an interview with their parents or carers.
- Each student could collect data from their parents using a standardised, self-complete questionnaire.

Think about the advantages and disadvantages of each of these methods and **note your thoughts in the table on page 14**.

Method	Advantages	Problems
Write recollections		
Interview parents		
Questionnaire		

You may have identified some of the following problems:

- Memories of early childhood are often poor or non-existent and the data obtained may be patchy or inaccurate.
- Face-to-face interviews would be time consuming (and could be potentially embarrassing!).
- It would be difficult to ensure that each student asked the same questions in the same way to produce comparable data.

For these reasons, you are going to construct a questionnaire that will allow you to collect data quickly, with the same questions being asked of all parents/carers so that answers can be easily compared.

Surveys/questionnaires are not like experiments as you will not have an independent or dependent variable. You are not looking for differences between conditions, you are looking to describe the day-care experiences of your group and the reasons for parents' choices, making this a descriptive survey. That is why you are using research questions rather than hypotheses.

Step 2 Consider ethical issues

Think about the ethical issues involved in this piece of research. Parents/carers will be completing a questionnaire about the type of day care used and the reasons for this. It may be a sensitive topic so be careful to respect people's views, opinions and experiences.

- Some members of your group may not live with their birth family. They may have been in state care or be unable to access data about their early childhood. For this reason (or any other), they may choose not to supply data for this practical.
- An important principle of research is to enable participants to give their informed consent to take part. This rule applies whoever you are collecting data from, including family and friends. You will need to inform participants that the study involves questions about their choice of day care and roughly how long the study will take. **Construct an information sheet** to do this. The consent form should make it clear that they are free to withdraw from the study at any time. **Adapt the consent form in the Appendix** for your study.

- Another important ethical principle is the need for confidentiality. You should ensure that the questionnaires do not allow people to be identified. Codes and numbers instead of names are generally a good way of achieving this.

- Participants should be debriefed after they have taken part in data collection. Make a debriefing sheet and provide it to participants after they have taken part. Ask whether they have questions about the study and answer the questions (or try to find answers to them). Debriefing is a way of ensuring that your participants go away feeling as good as when they started and understand what the research was about.

Step 3 *Sampling*

In this study, the sample type has already been decided for you. However, it is useful to reflect on the type of sample you are using. This is an opportunity sample as the data will be collected from people who are quickly and easily available – families of classmates.

Think about the advantages and disadvantages of opportunity sampling and record them below.

> *Advantages and disadvantages of opportunity sampling:*
> _____
> _____
> _____
> _____

> **Look it up …**
>
> Remind yourself about the advantages and disadvantages of opportunity sampling. Look at your AS Student Book or another resource.

Step 4 *Designing your questionnaire and standardised instructions*

In a questionnaire, people are asked for their views on a specific topic and the same questions are used for everyone.

Construct a questionnaire. It should take no longer than about five minutes to answer your questionnaire and the questions used must be clear, straightforward and easy to understand. Avoid jargon or terms that are difficult to understand and aim for clarity.

Your questionnaire should cover the following topic areas:

1 Whether the child attended day care before starting school.

2 What the type(s) of day care was.

3 The child's age when they started day care.

4 How long and how frequently they attended each day or week.

5 The factors that influenced the choice of day care.

6 Whether the child seemed to enjoy day care and their likes or dislikes about it.

7 The benefits of the child attending day care.

8 The kinds of activities provided in the day-care setting.

You could share the topic areas between groups so that each group composes questions relating to their allocated topics. The questions will then be compiled into one questionnaire for everybody in the group to use, so the data collected will be comparable.

Questionnaires can use open or closed questions depending on the type of information sought.

Question type	Description	Example
Open question	A question that asks the respondent to compose an answer in their own words	What reasons influenced your choice of day care?
Closed question	The respondent chooses one option from a list of pre-set answers (or they choose either yes or no)	Did your child attend: a) nursery; b) childminder; or c) was looked after by relatives?

Closed questions are best used for topics when there are a small number of potential answers, for example about types of care. It is easy to compare answers given by different people and to summarise the findings using percentages and graphs, for example how many people attended nursery and how many went to a childminder. **Prepare closed questions for topics 1, 2, 3 and 4 in the list on page 15.**

Open questions are useful when you want to gather detailed information about something in the participant's own words. For this reason, you should **prepare open questions for topics 5, 6, 7 and 8**. It will be harder to compare answers to these questions as people may talk about very different things in response to them. You need to **write standard instructions for how to fill in the questionnaire** and include them with it.

Step 5 *Piloting*

A pilot study is the last stage of planning before any real data are collected. It enables you to check that your materials, instructions and procedures work smoothly. **Try the questionnaire on one or two people** including the materials, such as the instructions to use it. Make sure the questions make sense without you having to explain any of them. You might have to amend your materials or procedure from what you find from the pilot. Ideally, the participant in your pilot study should be someone who has children who have attended day care, but if this is not possible, you could trial the materials on anyone who was not involved in producing them.

> **Look it up ...**
>
> Refresh your memory about the precise differences between open and closed questions and the advantages and disadvantages of each.

> **Ethical issues**
>
> If the parents or carers involved choose not to provide information then they should feel free to withdraw from participation, and this should not be questioned by others. The identities of those who chose not to participate do not need to be revealed (they have the right to anonymity).

Record any problems or changes needed to your questionnaire and instructions here:

_____

_____

_____

Step 6 *Collecting and pooling the data*

When the questionnaire is constructed, each student should take a copy and collect data from *one* of their parents/carers to avoid duplication of information. Ask them to complete the questionnaire as well as they can and remind them not to write names or details that will allow families to be identified. Pool the responses within your class. Everyone needs a copy of all of the data that come back. How you do this might depend on your group size. Details of how to collate and record the data are provided in the next steps.

Step 7 *Display your data using tables and graphs*

Analyse the data for each question separately. Data from the closed questions (1, 2, 3 and 4) can easily be converted into quantitative form by counting how many people chose each option. Display these in a table similar to the one below using total scores or percentages. You can also calculate some descriptive statistics to summarise the data, for example the mean age at which your group started nursery. You can then display your data using graphs if you wish. Pie charts are a useful way of demonstrating how a whole data set is divided into parts. Bar charts can also be used to compare classes or groups of data. Your graphs could be drawn on graph paper or presented using a program such as Excel.

Types of day care attended

	Number	Percentage
Nursery	11	50%
Childminder	3	14%
Relative	5	22%
Mixture of day-care settings	3	14%

Pie chart: Types of day care

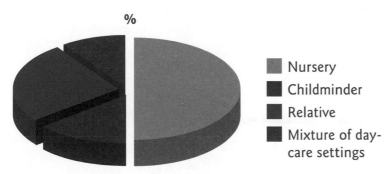

%

- Nursery
- Childminder
- Relative
- Mixture of day-care settings

Step 8 *Analysing your qualitative data*

Questions 5, 6, 7 and 8 will have produced qualitative data in the form of written answers. Collate the answers to each of these questions separately by listing them on separate sheets. You can then look through each set of answers and identify common answers that are similar and belong together. Give them a code or a descriptive label.

Example: In response to the question 'What factors influenced your choice of day care?' the following answers were given:

The nursery was just down the road.

My sister's little girl went there, so she could drop them both off together.

The childminder lived very close to my husband's office.

These responses all refer to how easy it was to use the day-care facility and could be coded as 'convenience'.

Conclude your project by returning to the two research questions posed at the start:

- What types of day care did students attend and for how long?
- What factors influenced the choices that the parents/carers made about day care?

Summarise answers to both of these questions clearly and succinctly.

Critical discussion

Methodology

- Was your questionnaire a useful way of collecting descriptive data?
- Were any of the questions problematic? Which ones were problematic and why?
- Were parents able to remember the information that you asked them for?
- Can you suggest any ways the practical could be improved?

Ethics

- Did your study throw up any unseen ethical issues?
- How did people feel about taking part?
- What have you learned about research with people?

References

Melhuish, E.C. (1990) Research on day care for young children in the UK. In E.C. Melhuish and P. Moss (eds) *Day care for young children: International perspectives*. London: Routledge.

Developmental psychology

4 Institutional care

> **Learning outcomes for this practical**
> - A3, B6, C1, C4, C5

Hint
Check these learning outcomes against the list on pages iv–v.

Student practical

In this practical you are going to analyse interviews that have been especially constructed for this book. These interviews concern the progress of young children from Romanian orphanages who have been adopted by UK families. This practical is different to the other activities in this workbook as you will not be collecting data. Instead, the main focus will be on developing and practising your analytical skills. After you have analysed the data, you will need to compare your findings with those of another student in order to check for reliability.

Background

It is widely accepted that the first few years of a child's life are important for later emotional development. Attachments with carers provide children with security and enable them to explore the world and learn about their surroundings. However, some children experience difficult circumstances and have little opportunity to form attachments.

In the 1990s, the civil war in Romania led to thousands of babies and infants spending time in dirty cots in deprived institutions with minimal human contact. Some of these children have been adopted by British and Canadian families and their progress is being tracked through ongoing case studies.

Case studies are detailed sets of information gathered about an individual or a small group of people. They include information gathered from interviews with a range of different people and are typically carried out longitudinally, with researchers returning to interview participants at regular intervals.

Case studies have provided very useful information in helping us to understand the long-term effects of early privation and institutionalisation on young children. You may be familiar with the case studies reported by Koluchova (1972 and 1991) of twin boys and by Skuse (1984) of Mary and Louise. These studies have shown that children can recover from adverse circumstances if good care is provided.

Interviews and case studies provide an effective way of gaining insight into the personal experiences of the families involved in adopting children who have been in institutions. They have also been helpful for challenging some of the claims of attachment theory, notably the idea that attachments must be formed within a 'critical period'.

Key study

Adopted Romanian orphans, Chisholm *et al.* (1997)

Chisholm *et al.* (1997) carried out a study of adopted Romanian orphans to assess possible problems in development. Three groups of children were compared:

- One group of 46 children had spent at least eight months in a Romanian orphanage before adoption. This group were referred to as Romanian orphans (RO).

- One group of 46 children had been brought up in Canadian families with no experience of adoption or institutionalisation. This group were referred to as Canadian born (CB) and acted as a control group.

- A group of 29 children were adopted from Romania before the age of four months and had little or no orphanage experience. This group were referred to as Romanian controls (RC).

The children were compared for the incidence of medical and behavioural problems. Data was gathered through interviews with the children's parents who were asked to describe any difficulties they had experienced with their children. Parents also completed a structured questionnaire called the Child Behaviour Checklist.

Chisholm *et al.* found that parents of the RO orphans reported significantly more eating problems (notably eating too much or refusing solid food) and medical/health difficulties than the other two groups. They also showed more stereotyped behaviours such as rocking backwards and forwards. Parents were also more likely than the other groups to report that their children had difficulty making friends. However, there was no difference in the number of children with sleeping problems in the three groups.

Ethical issues

In this exercise, ethical issues have been dealt with by providing you with data that has been fabricated (the interviews are not real). This removes the problem of obtaining informed consent and maintaining confidentiality/anonymity, which would be necessary if you were to analyse data from real interviews. However, you will gain just as much experience of the processes involved in analysis as you would with genuine data.

Method

Step 1 *The design of the study*

In this study, the data collection has already been carried out and you will implement a method of analysis. The data provided consist of written transcripts of interviews with two couples who had each adopted a Romanian child from an impoverished institution. The interviews were carried out within the parents' own home and both members of the couple were present. Each parent was asked the same question, which was:

'What difficulties did your child experience in the first months and what benefits has the adoption brought to your family?'

Their answers were recorded and transcribed (written out exactly) providing qualitative data. The interview transcripts are in the Appendix on pages 59–61.

Qualitative data can be analysed in a range of different ways. Two of the most common ways for interviews are:

- Content analysis: this method involves counting the number of references within the transcript to topics defined before the research takes place in the hypothesis or research question. For example, researchers could count the number of references to difficulties or problems with the children. This method converts the qualitative data into quantitative format by counting.
- Thematic analysis: this method does not attempt to reduce the data to quantitative format through counting. Instead, the research looks for themes that recur in the narratives and summarises the main themes using quotations from the evidence as support. This does not reduce the data to quantitative format.

Remember that a research question is more open than a hypothesis and does not make a prediction. Research questions are often used in interviews and qualitative work.

In this study, you are going to use the first method outlined above – content analysis. You are going to build on Chisholm's work by considering the difficulties experienced by institutionalised children when they arrived from Romania. You are also going to develop this further by considering the benefits that the children bring to their new families.

You will focus your analysis on two research questions (or RQs):

- RQ1: 'What difficulties did the adoptive children experience in the first months with their new families?
- RQ2: 'What benefits do adopted children bring to their new families?'

> **Look it up ...**
>
> Remind yourself of qualitative data by looking in your AS Student Book or another resource.

Step 2 Preparing for analysis

The first stage of analysis of qualitative data is familiarisation. This involves reading through the interview transcripts two or three times without preconceived ideas about what you might find. You might find it useful to keep a pen handy and make a note of your thoughts about the interviews.

Now think about your research question. You will need to decide what you are going to count or code. Research question 1 is focused on the difficulties reported by parents, so this should form the basis of your analysis. The most common method of devising categories is to use the findings from previous research studies. Chisholm *et al.* (1997) found that parents reported children having difficulties with eating, relationships with siblings or peers, stereotypical behaviours and medical/health problems, but no problems with sleeping. As you want to compare your findings with Chisholm *et al.*, these five categories (including sleeping) should be used to code the data.

For each category, you will need to record how many times it is mentioned in all the interviews. Remember that the actual words used may not be the same as the category title. A parent may say that a child 'does not sleep well' or 'will not go to bed' rather than referring to sleeping difficulties, so you will have to think carefully about how to code each reference to a problem.

Create a data record sheet similar to the one below. This will allow you to record references to each category in each of the four interviews.

Category	Sue	David	Peter	Safi
Health problems				
Sleeping problems				
Eating problems				
Difficulties with peers or siblings				
Stereotypical behaviours				

Research question 2 is a little different as you are not aware of previous research into the benefits of adoption so you cannot use existing categories for coding. In order to code these data, you should **devise your own categories from the data provided.** You can do this by reading the interviews and noting down all of the benefits mentioned. When you have done this, you should check to see whether there are benefits that are logically similar and can be grouped together. These 'groups' are your categories that will be used for coding. **Write your categories in here and put these into a data record sheet similar to the one above.**

Categories:

_____

_____

_____

Step 3 *Coding the data*

Read through the interview transcripts again and code the data. Work through each category one at a time and pick out all of the references to it that you can find in the four interviews. You can underline these on the transcript itself or highlight them using a different colour for each. **Enter your data onto your two data record sheets.**

Step 4 *Compare your findings/check for reliability*

One of the features of qualitative data is that they are more subjective (open to interpretation) than quantitative measures. If you have measured time taken to complete a task in seconds, it is likely that your measurement will be identical to that of someone else measuring the same thing, and that makes it reliable. However, when analysing verbal data from interviews it is much harder to be objective. You are likely to bring your own interpretation to the words and statements in the interviews.

You should compare your findings with at least one other person who has done the same exercise. In order for your coding to be classed as reliable, you should largely agree on the frequency of each category for RQ1. If you recorded very different scores, go back to your interview transcripts and compare your analysis. You have probably interpreted statements in the interviews differently and coded them into different categories. Discuss each difference and decide which interpretation is the best. The more points that you agree on, the more reliable your analysis is.

Critical discussion

Theory

- What kinds of difficulties were referred to most commonly by the four parents in this study?
- Did your findings support those of Chisholm or did they contradict them?
- If your findings were different to those of Chisholm, can you think of reasons why this might be?
- Which were the most common benefits reported by parents?

Methodology

- What are the some of the difficulties of working with qualitative data?
- Did you find close agreement with another coder in your class?
- How easy was it to devise the categories from the data for RQ2? Was it difficult to code the data into these categories?
- One criticism of content analysis is that it reduces the rich data provided by interviews. Did you see that as a problem?
- Can you suggest any ways the practical could be improved?

References

Fisher, L., Ames, E.W., Chisholm, K. and Savoie, L. (1997) Problems Reported by Parents of Romanian Orphans Adopted to British Columbia. *International Journal of Behavioural Development*, **20**(1), 67–82.

Koluchova, J. (1991) Severely deprived twins after 22 years of observation. *Studia Psychologica*, **33**, 23–8.

Skuse, D. (1984) Extreme deprivation in early childhood – II. Theoretical issues and a comparative review. *Journal of Child Psychology and Psychiatry*, **25**(4), 543–72.

Biological psychology

5 | Type A behaviour

Learning outcomes for this practical

- A5, A6, B2, B3, B4, B5, B7, B9, B10 , C2, C3, C5, C7

Hint

Check these learning outcomes against the list on pages iv–v.

Student practical

This practical is an observation. You will create a mildly stressful situation and observe the frequency of Type A behaviours. You will also ask participants to fill in a Type A/Type B personality questionnaire. This will allow you to see whether the behaviours observed correspond to the participants' personality type as identified by the test.

Background

In simple terms, stress is defined as feeling under pressure or struggling to cope with the demands of the environment. Everyone experiences stress at different points in their life. A glance around your classmates or family will remind you that people respond very differently to stress. While some people seem to thrive on stressful situations, others dislike stress and avoid it as much as possible. Then there are those lucky people who appear to be completely laid-back and not register stress at all.

Why do people respond so differently to stressful situations? The answer to this is complex and relates to both the nature of the stressful event and factors within the individual. In this practical, you are interested in factors within the individual – sometimes called individual differences or personality. The study of human personality is complicated, with many different theories and approaches, but an influential idea relating to stress is the concept of Type A personality also known as Type A behaviour pattern (TABP). The TABP was first identified by two cardiologists, Friedman and Rosenman, working in California in the 1950s. Friedman and Rosenman noticed how many of their patients appeared to have a similar type of personality. They defined Type A personality as a behaviour pattern characterised by time pressure, competitiveness and hostility. You can see a more detailed explanation of these three qualities in the table opposite.

Behaviour pattern	Examples
Time pressure	Type A people work to deadlines and typically do several things at once. They are always busy and are unhappy doing nothing. They typically walk and eat quickly.
Competitive	Type A people want to achieve and aim to come first. They are highly competitive in sport, work and play.
Hostility	Type A people tend to get angry and impatient with others. They also become angry with themselves when they get things wrong or do not do well.

Type Bs are basically the opposite of the Type As. They tend to take things more slowly and are much less worried about time. They talk, walk and eat more slowly. They finish one job before moving on to the next and they avoid doing several things at once. They tend to be less impatient with themselves and other people and are happy to let other people win.

These different behaviours are thought to relate to health. Rosenman *et al.* (1976) carried out a series of studies in California collectively known as the Western Collaborative Group studies. These studies set out to assess the relationship between personality type and health, mainly through rates of heart disease. They developed a method of assessing personality type using a structured interview.

Key study

Rosenman *et al.* (1976), the assessment of Type A behaviour

Rosenman *et al.* (1976) studied over 3,000 middle-aged men living in California. In order to assess whether they were Type A or Type B personality, each participant took part in a structured interview. In the interview, the researchers asked questions about behaviour and recorded the answers. In addition, they observed the participant's behaviour when the situation was mildly frustrating, for example when the questions were asked rather slowly. Rosenman noted down behavioural signals that showed Type A characteristics, such as impatience (finger tapping or interrupting) or time pressure (rapid speech).

Using the data gathered from the structured interview, the researchers classified each participant into either Type A behaviour pattern or Type B behaviour pattern. The men were followed up for eight-and-a-half years to assess their health and the incidence of heart disease. During this time, 257 men experienced heart attacks. Of these, 69 per cent were people who had been categorised as Type A, leading the researchers to conclude that the Type A personality is a major risk factor for heart disease in the middle-aged.

Since then, doubt has been cast on their findings by studies that have found little difference in heart disease rates between Type A and Type B people (e.g. Shekelle *et al.*, 1985). However, subsequent research has indicated that the trait of hostility is the aspect of personality most closely associated with heart disease (Dembrowski *et al.*, 1989; Miller *et al.*, 1996).

Although their original ideas have been developed and modified, the concept of TABP has continued to be influential in the study of individual differences and stress. In this practical, you are going to use the method of observation to study the behaviour of a small number of people by recording their behavioural responses to a mildly challenging situation. You will then compare this with scores from a Type A and Type B questionnaire. Because this topic needs careful ethical consideration, ethical issues are covered in Step 1 below.

Method

Step 1 *Ethical issues*

Ethical issues guide practical choices and decisions at all stages of the research process. Think about the ethical issues involved in this piece of research. You want to examine behaviours and responses to mildly stressful situations. Theoretically, you could investigate differences in response to stress by observing people in naturally occurring stressful situations such as waiting to start an exam or driving test or in the dentist's waiting room, but this would pose ethical difficulties. Observing people in these situations without their consent would be unacceptable and many people would not consent to being observed when they are already feeling stressed.

It is important that the situation you use does not cause distress to participants or be experienced as more than mildly stressful. For this reason, you should use a puzzle or conundrum similar to the brain teasers used in papers and magazines. These puzzles are no more stressful than many activities students experience in everyday life, making it suitable for your purposes.

You should choose one of the suggestions here or find one that will do the job just as well. The puzzle needs to be impossible to complete, but that should not be obvious. Some options are:

- redraw the puzzle at www.jimloy.com/puzz/puzzle.htm and give the instructions with it
- use the animals or vegetables word search at www.chrisdunmire.com/fun/worlds.hardest.puzzles.shtml.

Another alternative would be to create a large word-search puzzle yourself and get participants to look for words that are not present.

- An important principle of research is to enable participants to give their fully informed consent to take part. However, in studies of this nature, informing participants in detail about the nature of the research is likely to lead to demand characteristics, which enable the participant to work out the 'correct' way to behave and produces unrealistic or socially desirable behaviour. For example, telling participants that the puzzle is impossible at the start will defeat the purpose of the study.

- For this reason, you should ask your participants for consent to take part and provide some of the details of the study while withholding others. You should tell them that the study involves trying to solve a difficult puzzle and that it

Look it up …

You might want to remind yourself about the processes involved in controlled observation. Ainsworth's study of the Strange Situation is a good example of controlled observation even though it deals with the topic of attachment types in young children.

will take around five minutes. You should also inform them that you would like to watch their behaviour while they are doing the puzzle. However, you will withhold information about the precise details of the study until after it is completed.

- You should also ask for their consent to fill in a questionnaire.

- At the end of your study you will debrief your participants, explaining to them that you have been observing their behaviour under mildly stressful situations. Give them the right to withdraw their data from the study. This is known as retrospective informed consent. You will need to produce a standard debriefing sheet to give to participants at the end of the study. Remember that the questionnaire will produce a Type A/Type B score and this will need to be explained in the debriefing.

- Ensure that you record data about your participants in an anonymous form, using initials or numbers so they cannot be identified .This is good ethical practice.

Step 2 *Choosing a type of observation and personality test*

The next step in the research process is to choose a suitable method to investigate the topic of interest. Here, the topic of interest is individual differences in behaviour in response to mildly stressful situations. Your method is controlled observation.

In a controlled observation, the researcher controls certain aspects of the environment, often to make things happen. This is useful in speeding up the pace of research and it is in contrast to naturalistic observation, in which a researcher observes naturally occurring behaviour. You are using controlled observation by setting up the mildly challenging situation with the puzzle. This will enable you to observe the different ways that people react.

As well as distinguishing between controlled and naturalistic observation, you can also distinguish between structured and unstructured observation. The terms 'structured observation' and 'unstructured observation' refer to how the data are collected and recorded. In a structured observation, the data are collected using a preprepared data collection grid in which behaviours are counted as they are seen occurring. This is suitable for your purposes, as you want to record precise behaviours that demonstrate TABP, and you can decide on these before you collect the data.

You should also identify an online Type A/Type B personality questionnaire for participants to complete after they have taken part in the observation. There are a number of different tests for Type A/Type B personality and you will need to choose one carefully. Firstly, you need to identify one that gives a score rather than just a description of personality type. Secondly, you need to identify one that does not take up too much of your participants' time. There are some short questionnaires that can be downloaded from the internet as pdf documents. These may be more convenient for both the participant and you as the investigator. See for example www.elibay.com/assets/files/typeA.pdf.

Step 3 *Operationalising key variables for the observation*

In this practical you are not making a prediction about differences or relationships between variables. **Your aim is to observe and record, accurately and reliably, the response to stress and to compare this with findings from the questionnaire.** This is not an experiment or a correlational study and this means that you will not have a hypothesis. However, when you measure a variable (in this case Type A behaviour) you need to define it precisely. This process of defining variables is known as operationalisation. In simple terms, operationalisation means stating exactly what you want to observe and measure.

Think carefully about what is meant by the word 'behaviour'. When you say someone is impatient, you are making a judgement about their behaviour, but you cannot actually *see* impatience. Behaviour refers to actions that can be seen and counted. It is possible to distinguish between non-verbal behaviour (body language) and verbal behaviour (what is said and how it is said).

In this practical you want to **operationalise the Type A behaviour pattern**, which has three components: time pressure, competitiveness and hostility. The first of these is the easiest to spot in behaviour so you should focus on that. What kinds of behaviours indicate time pressure? Rosenman *et al.* noted a number of different signs including interruption of other people, rate (speed) of speech, using hand gestures (gesticulating), finger tapping and facial tension. The first two of these signs relate to verbal behaviour and are not directly relevant to this situation. Other kinds of non-verbal behaviour that might indicate time pressure in this context could include tongue clicking, tapping the computer keyboard or desk, repeated fiddling with phone, biting nails, knee jiggling or foot tapping. You may be able to think of other behaviour that indicates time pressure.

In observational studies, researchers make decisions about the most useful behaviours to record as it is difficult to observe and count accurately more than five or six behaviours. Discuss the above options and your own suggestions and decide which behaviours you will look for and record.

> **Look it up ...**
>
> You might want to refresh your memory about the importance of operationalisation by looking back at your AS Student Book or other resources.

Record your decisions here.

_____

_____

_____

_____

_____

_____

Create an observation record and standardised instructions

Now you need to create a structured observation grid that shows your chosen behaviours. You should list these across the top of the grid and put the *initials* of your participants down the left-hand side (see the grid below). This will ensure that the participants' anonymity is maintained. This grid will enable you to tick the behaviours each time you see them occurring – a method called 'event sampling'.

Participant	Finger tapping	Knee jiggling	Fiddling with phone	Biting nails	Hand gestures	Tapping keyboard
L.H.	|||		||||			||||
P.T.	|	||		|	|	

You also need to write a list of standardised instructions for your participants that tell them clearly what you want them to do with the puzzle. You should inform them how much time they will have for the activity and remind them that they will be fully debriefed at the end of the study.

The questionnaire you have chosen should contain standard instructions about how to complete it. However, these probably will not inform participants that they are free to withdraw from the study and you should add that information.

Step 5 *Sampling*

Select a sample of people to take part in your study. Your participants can be adults of any age, but avoid asking people that you know are currently under stress. You should also check that the potential participants are comfortable using a computer keyboard and mouse if you are using a computer-based test.

In order to have sufficient data to analyse, you should aim to gather data from around five participants. You should aim for a similar number of men and women in your sample.

There are three types of sample that you are required to know about:

- a random sample
- an opportunity sample
- a self-selected (volunteer) sample.

Think about the advantages and disadvantages of each of these types of sample and decide which method you intend to use. Record this below.

> **Look it up ...**
>
> You might want to remind yourself about sampling methods by looking at your AS Student Book or other resources.

Chosen sampling method and reasons for choice:

_____

_____

_____

_____

Step 6 *Piloting*

A pilot study is the last stage of planning, before real data is collected. It is an important process in an observational study as it allows you to assess the behaviours you have included on your grid to see whether they are workable. It also enables you to check that your materials, instructions and procedure work smoothly and amend them if necessary. You should aim to test a couple of people, starting with consent and instructions and debriefing them at the end. As part of the debriefing, you should ask participants about their feelings while they were doing the puzzle. This enables you to check that the procedure does cause mild, but not undue, stress.

Think about how and where you will collect your data. The environment you use should be kept the same (as much as is practically possible) for all of the participants.

You should think about the amount of time you have given them to attempt the puzzle and assess whether it is too short or too long.

During your pilot, experiment with where to sit while you are recording your data. This should preferably be somewhere where you can see your participant clearly but where you will not distract them or put them off.

Finally, you should ask your participants to complete the Type A/Type B questionnaire. Check whether your participants understand the instructions about the questionnaire. Note the time it takes them to complete the questionnaire so that you can give a rough guide in the consent form.

Make sure that the participants in the pilot know that they cannot talk to other participants about the study until after those people have taken part in it.

> *Record any changes needed to the behaviours included on your observation grid.*
>
> _____
>
> _____
>
> _____
>
> _____
>
> _____
>
> _____

When you are satisfied that your procedures work satisfactorily, collect data from five or six people.

> **Think about it**
>
> You may find that you change some aspects of your study after the pilot. This could include your instructions or the behaviours you have included in your structured observation grid.

Analysing your data

Step 7 *Descriptive analysis and display of data using graphs and charts*

You should have a completed data sheet that contains a tally of the number of times each behaviour was shown by each of your participants. You can simplify and summarise your raw data using tables.

Firstly, calculate the total number of Type A behaviours shown for each participant. Display these using a table similar to the one below, showing the highest total for an individual through to the lowest total so that you can look at the pattern. In the next line of the table, insert the questionnaire score for each participant.

Participant	1	2	3	4	5	6
Total Type A behaviours	16	14	11	7	4	3
Questionnaire score	105	112	88	42	54	20

One way of finding out whether the observed behaviour shows a similar pattern of results to the questionnaire scores is to draw a scattergram like the one below. This shows whether there is a relationship, or correlation between the two measures.

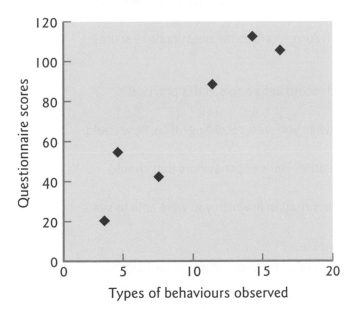

Scattergram of number of observed Type A behaviours and questionnaire score

You can also calculate the totals of each kind of behaviour from the observations. This information will tell you which kinds of behaviours are most commonly shown when people experience mildly stressful tasks. In the example on page 32, finger tapping and knee jiggling were the most common signs of time pressure. Nail biting was the least common.

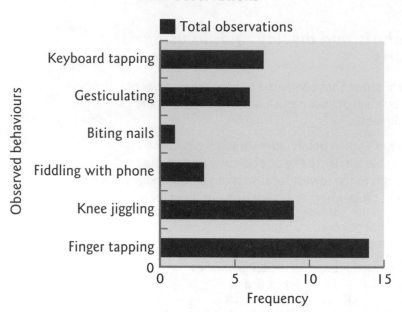

Total observations

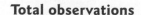

Think about validity

Here, you used a frustrating puzzle as the task to elicit a mild degree of stress. How realistic was this as a way of measuring responses to stress?

Critical discussion

Theory

- Did your analysis support the idea that people differ in their response to stress?

- Did your participants fall clearly into Type A or Type B patterns or were most of them somewhere in-between?

- Did the observed behaviour pattern correspond to the questionnaire score?

Methodology

- How difficult was it to observe and record behaviours in this practical exercise?

- Did you miss some of the actions while you were recording? If so, how could you improve this?

- Did your participants demonstrate other kinds of behaviours that should have been included on your grid?

- Did the puzzle task create a realistic situation in which you were able to see responses to mild stress?

- Were your standardised instructions clear?

- Was the personality questionnaire suitable for your sample of participants?

Ethics

- How did your participants feel about taking part when they were told that the puzzle was insolvable?

- Did anyone choose to withdraw their data in this study?

- What have you learned about research with people?

References

Dembrowski, T.M., MacDougal, J.M., Costa, P.T., and Grandits, G.A. (1989) Components of hostility as predictors of sudden death and myocardial infarction in the Multiple Risk Factor Intervention Trial. *Psychosomatic Medicine*, **51**, 514–22.

Miller, T.Q., Smith, T.W., Turner, C.W., Guijarro, M.L. and Hallet, A.J. (1996) A meta-analytic review of research on hostility and physical health. *Psychological Bulletin*, **119**, 322–48.

Rosenman, R.H., Brand, R.J., Sholtz, R.I. and Friedman, M. (1976) Multivariate prediction of coronary heart disease during 8.5-year follow-up in the Western Collaborative Group study. *The American Journal of Cardiology*, **37**, 903–10.

Shekelle, R.B., Hulley, S.B. and Neaton, J.D. (1985) The MRFIT behaviour pattern study II. Type A behaviour and incidence of coronary heart disease. *American Journal of Epidemiology*, **122**, 559–70.

Biological psychology

6 | Measuring stress

Learning outcomes for this practical

- A1, A4, A6, B1, B2, B4, B5, C2, C3, C5, C7

Hint

Check these learning outcomes against the list on pages iv–v.

Student practical

In this practical you are going to adapt a scale to investigate stress levels in students. This exercise will work best if you perform it in small groups to collect and analyse ratings of events that are related to stress in students.

Background

Stress is part of everyone's life. Sometimes stress comes from minor events such as missing the bus. Sometimes people experience stress because of long-term factors such as impending examinations, the inability to cope with the demands of a job, or chronic illness. Stress comes from many sources, and many events that happen in our lives add to our stress. Traumatic events such as the death of a loved one cause great stress, but even events that should be pleasurable, such as getting married or Christmas, can be stressful.

Psychologists have devised a number of ways of assessing individual levels of stress, but all of the methods suffer from methodological problems. One of these problems is operationalising the concept of stress. Everyone has a notion of what stress is, but it is a difficult concept to measure. For example, should you measure the total of what a person has to deal with in their life (an objective measure) or the person's belief about how well they are coping with these demands (a subjective measure)? Another problem is that for ethical reasons it is not possible to study stress experimentally and therefore observation, interview or survey designs have to be used.

Holmes and Rahe (1967) devised the social readjustment rating scale (SRRS). It used self-reports of the major life events that had affected people as an objective measure of their stress levels. They drew up a list of life events that might affect adults during their lives, such as divorce, getting a new job or a son/daughter leaving home, and they asked a large group of people to rate these against the adjustment needed after marriage. Each of the events, or 'life change units', was assigned an average score ranging from 100 for death of a spouse to 50 for marriage and 11 for minor violations of the law. The score from the scale was arrived at simply by adding the scores for all of the events that had affected an individual during the past two years. Studies have shown that high scores are associated with a much greater risk of stress-related illnesses.

Look it up ...

Remind yourself about methods of measuring stress in everyday life by looking at your AS Student Book or another resource.

There are a number of problems with using the SRRS as a measure of stress levels. One is that it assumes that any particular event has an equal impact on all people. However, this is clearly not the case. For example, pregnancy is given a rating of 40, but the impact on a woman depends on whether she wants a child or not, financial circumstances, and so on. One way of investigating the effect of events on individuals is to use structured interviews.

Another criticism of the SRRS is that it focuses on major life events but not the everyday events that seem to be the trigger for many people's feelings of stress. This was addressed by Kanner *et al.* (1981), who devised a scale designed to measure the effect of daily 'hassles' and 'uplifts'. It is called the hassles and uplifts scale (HSUP).

Key study

Comparison of two modes of stress measurement: Daily hassles and uplifts versus major life events. Kanner, Coyne, Schaefer and Lazarus (1981)

Kanner *et al.* (1981) believed that although life events have an impact on stress levels, for many people it is the cumulative effect of day-to-day problems that is the major influence on stress and stress-related illnesses. They devised a scale to measure these daily events. The scale consisted of 53 items. Some of the items referred to daily hassles that they characterised as being the irritating, frustrating or distressing demands found with everyday transactions. Other items were daily uplifts, or positive experiences. Participants were asked to indicate to what degree each event had been part of their life in the past month.

The scale was given to a community sample of adults once a month for 10 months. Kanner *et al.* claimed that the HSUP was a better predictor of psychological symptoms than the life events scores. They concluded that HSUP was better at predicting stress than the life event approach.

The HSUP scale was a significant development in research of the effect of everyday events on levels of stress. However, subsequent research has suggested that the HSUP scale did not place enough emphasis on the positive and negative impact of interpersonal events (Maybery and Graham, 2001).

Maybery (2003, 2009) has developed a number of scales to measure the effect of both life and interpersonal events. These are called the Positive Event Scale (PES) and the Negative Event Scale (NES). There are two versions of both the PES and the NES – one for university students and another for middle-aged adults. All scales have proved to be reliable and valid in tests of more than 1,600 participants.

In this practical you will adapt the items on the university student NES (see the Appendix, pages 62–4). The aim is to make it applicable to your student population and to use the scale to assess the number of stress-related events affecting a sample of students.

Method

Step 1 *Design your study*

The first step of the research process is to identify a topic of interest and to choose a suitable method to investigate it. Here, the topic of interest is the level of stress experienced in a student's life. The method you will use is a survey, using a questionnaire of a specific type called a scale.

In this practical you will be using closed questions that give a quantitative measure of stress. Very clear instructions must be provided about how to complete the survey and it must ask questions that all participants can understand.

When the purpose of the questionnaire is to provide a scale or measure of a particular behaviour, it may take many years to refine it to improve its reliability and validity. For this reason, it is always best to use a questionnaire that has already been tested and validated. This is particularly useful when researching a complex topic such as stress. You will use the NES for university students mentioned above. It can be found in the Appendix on pages 62–4 or as a pdf document at www.quantifyingconnections.com by clicking on the 'Positive and negative event scales' link. This shows information about how the scale was developed and allows you to download the NES from the 'Negative Event (hassle) Scale for University Students' link in that page.

The NES contains a few questions that are unlikely to have an effect on many AS level students such as questions 18–20 dealing with problems with children. These questions could be adapted to be more relevant to AS student life.

Step 2 *Ethical issues*

Ethical issues guide practical choices and decisions at all stages of the research process. Think about the ethical issues involved in this piece of research.

- An important principle of research is to enable participants to give their fully informed consent to take part. You should tell potential participants what is involved in the study, what they will be asked to do and roughly how long it will take. You should put this information in a consent form and present it to your participants to sign. The consent form should make it clear to your participants that they are free to withdraw at any time.

- You should ensure that your research does not make participants feel uncomfortable. This is particularly important when you are dealing with issues such as stress. Remember that you are asking about real events in students' lives and, although this is unlikely to add to feelings of stress or discomfort, you should be alert to the possibility and reiterate the right to withdraw if needed.

- The NES forms do not ask participants to give their name or any other details. If you adapt the scale, you should follow this example so that the questionnaires remain confidential.

- You will need to produce standard debriefing information to use at the end of the study. You should thank the participants and tell them about the aim of the study.

Step 3 *Sampling*

One of the aims of surveys that gather quantitative data is to be able to generalise the findings. This is only possible if there is a relatively large, representative sample. In this study your target population is AS and A2 students. You will need to consider how you can give the questionnaire to a large group of your peers in a way that is both practical and, most importantly, ethical.

You are required to know about three types of sample:

- a random sample
- an opportunity sample
- a self-selected (volunteer) sample.

Think about the advantages and disadvantages of each of these types of sample and decide which method you intend to use.

> **Look it up ...**
>
> You might want to remind yourself about the advantages and disadvantages of each of these sampling methods.

Chosen sample method:

_____

Step 4 *Create stimulus materials and questionnaires*

The first task is to adapt the NES with your small group of researchers. For example, items 18–20 refer to problems with children. These are problems that are likely to affect a small minority of your sample of AS and A level students and they could be replaced with three new items. The new items should not replicate any of the items already on the scale but they should be relevant to your cohort of 17–18-year-old students.

> **Think about it**
>
> You may find that you need to adapt the three new items after the pilot if your pilot group feel they are not relevant.

If you are using a volunteer sample and are making the questionnaire available to students (putting the materials somewhere volunteers can collect them rather than approaching potential participants), you will need to provide a pack containing the consent form, instructions and questionnaire. No matter how you obtain your sample, you should keep the signed consent forms separate from the responses to ensure confidentiality. It is good practice to put individual numbers on the response sheet that your participants can write down. This enables them to ask for their responses to be destroyed or returned if they wish to withdraw their data from the study later.

Most studies require you to devise a set of standardised instructions for your participants. However, the NES has a set of standard instructions that have already been piloted and used. You need to provide your participants with an information sheet explaining the purpose of the study and a consent form.

Step 5 *Piloting*

A pilot study is the last stage of planning before real data are collected. It enables you to check that your materials, instructions and procedures work smoothly. You should aim to pilot the questionnaire with three or four people, starting with consent and instructions, and then debriefing them at the end. The aim of the pilot is to check that all of the materials work and that they are understood by your student population.

Think about how and where you will collect your data. Remember that you may not be on hand when the participants in the main study complete their questionnaire. If there are questions about what to do, then the instructions are not sufficiently clear. These should be amended to improve clarity.

> *Record any problems or changes needed to your questionnaire or instructions here.*
>
> _____
>
> _____
>
> _____
>
> _____

Analysing your data

Step 6 *Descriptive analysis and display of data using graphs and charts*

Your NES or adapted scale for each participant consists of 57 items that are scored from 0 to 5. Zero is given if the event did not occur during the previous one-month period and 1 to 5 if it did. The 1 to 5 scores range from 1 if the event occurred but the participant did not experience any hassle, to 5 if the event occurred and the participant experienced extreme hassle.

The first stage of analysis is to sum the scores for the 57 items for each participant. This should give you a score from 0 (where a participant did not experience any of the events in the past month) to 285 (where a participant experienced every item and was extremely hassled by them all).

The individual scores for each participant need to be added to a tally chart or score sheet. Even if arranged in ascending order, this is likely to result in a confusing array of numbers because few, if any, of the participants will have the same scores. One way of dealing with this is to compile a frequency table. In the table you can record the number of people who have scores in a certain score band (e.g. 0–20, 21–40, as shown in the table below).

NES score	0–20	21–40	41–60	61–80	81–100	101–120	121–140	141–160	161–180	181–200
Number of participants	0	3	10	15	13	10	8	0	1	0

The size of the bands you choose will depend on the results. If the results have a large range, then the bands will need to be fairly large (as in the example above); but if there is a small range of scores, then the bands can be smaller.

The data in the table can be illustrated with a frequency diagram. This plots the score band on the horizontal axis and the number of people in each band, the frequency, on the vertical axis as shown in the graph below.

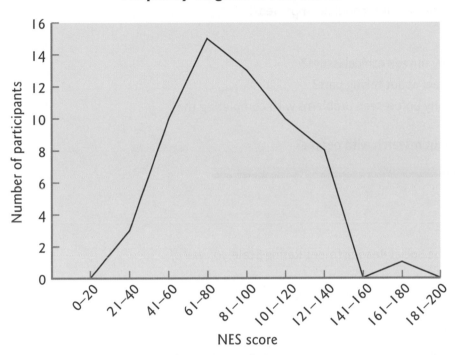

Frequency diagram of NES scores

You could analyse the results further by investigating the influence of different types of events. For example, questions 1–9, 25–40 and 45–48 are all concerned with interpersonal relationships, whereas the rest of the questions are not. Which set of questions is a major contributor to the scores in your sample? To analyse this, you will need to total the contribution of the two sets of items separately. If there are different numbers of questions in the sets (as with the above example), you will need to find the average for each grouping to compare them. Do this by dividing the total score for the set by the number of questions it contains.

Critical discussion

Theory
- Did your study fulfil the aim to investigate the types of life events that affect student stress levels?
- Do you think that knowing what events have affected an individual gives a good indication of their subjective feeling of stress?

Think about validity

You could have carried out this study using interviews about feelings of stress. Would this have given a more accurate picture of what your fellow students experience? Think of at least one ethical reason why this method was not suggested.

Methodology

- Did you have enough people to produce a representative picture of stressful events in a student's life?

- Was a questionnaire the best method of finding the levels of stress in students?

- Would an alternative method have revealed more detailed information?

- Were your standardised instructions clear?

- Can you suggest any ways the practical could be improved?

Ethics

- Did your study throw up any unseen ethical issues?

- How did your participants feel about taking part?

- Did your debriefing reveal any unforeseen problems with completing the questionnaire?

- What have you learned about research with people?

References

Holmes, T. and Rahe, R. (1967) The Social Readjustment Rating Scale. *Journal of Psychosomatic Research*, **II**, 213–8.

Kanner, A.D., Coyne, J.C., Schaefer, C. and Lazarus, R.S. (1981) Comparison of two modes of stress measurement: Daily hassles and uplifts versus major life events. *Journal of Behavioral Medicine*, **4**, 1–25.

Maybery, D.J. and Graham, D. (2001) Hassles and Uplifts: Including interpersonal events. *Stress and Health*, **17**, 91–104.

Maybery, D.J. (2003) Incorporating interpersonal events within hassle measurement. *Stress and Health*, **19**, 97–110.

Maybery, D.J. (2009) Hassles and Uplifts: Issues and Improvements in Measuring Day to Day Events. In P. Heidenreich and I. Prüter (eds) *Handbook of Stress: Causes, Effects and Control*. New York: Nova Science Publishers.

Social psychology

7   Social influence – class practical

> **Learning outcomes for this practical**
> - A6, B4, B5, B8, B9, B10, C2, C3, C5

> **Hint**
>
> Check these learning outcomes against the list on pages iv–v.

Class practical

Before working through this chapter, you should already have been a participant in the experiment described. This allows you to experience an experiment from the point of view of a participant before you carry out your own research. You can also look back at how the experiment was carried out and consider why this way of doing it (the method) was chosen.

If you have not taken part in an estimation experiment, please do not read the rest of the chapter yet. Knowing the full details of the study may alter your responses.

Background

Individuals are influenced by other people in a variety of ways. One of these social influences is conformity. Everybody conforms to their society or group norms to some extent, from stopping at a red light to listening to the same music and wearing the same clothes as their friends.

There are many types of conformity, such as compliance (behaving like others to fit in but not really agreeing) or identification (behaving like others because you identify with the group they are in). Another type is informational conformity. This happens when we are unsure of the answer so we look to others for information in order to be right. So, for example, if we do not know which knife and fork to use in a restaurant we look to see what other people are using and we do the same.

Some of the earliest social psychology studies investigated this type of conformity. For example, Jenness (1932) asked participants to estimate the number of beans in a jar. Most participants changed their individual estimate after a group discussion. Sherif (1936) investigated the 'autokinetic effect'. This happens when participants sit in a darkened room and stare at a pinpoint of light. Even though the light is still, it appears to move. Sherif's participants were unaware that the light was fixed and he asked them to estimate the distance it moved. The participants gave different estimates of the movement, but when they were put in rooms with others their estimates converged towards a group norm. Like Jenness, Sherif found that this group norm subsequently changed individual participant's estimates. This suggests that when people are put in a situation where the answer is not clear, they look to others for guidance. They adopt a group norm and show informational conformity. This practical exercise investigates informational conformity.

Key study

The role of discussion in changing opinion regarding matter of fact, Jenness (1932)

Jenness investigated informational conformity with a simple but effective experiment. He showed his participants a glass bottle filled with beans and asked them to estimate how many beans there were in the bottle. The participants' first estimate was an individual estimate and these tended to vary widely. Jenness then put his participants in a group and asked them to provide a group estimate after discussion. Finally, the participants were asked to give an individual estimate again.

Jenness found that the group discussion led to a consensus, but the interesting finding came from the second individual estimate. The majority of participants changed their original estimate to one that was closer to the group estimate. Their initial estimates had altered because of the influence of the majority opinion.

Method

Step 1   The design of the study: variables and hypotheses

The first step of the research process is to identify a topic of interest and to choose a suitable method to investigate it. In the class practical, the method used was an experiment.

In an experiment, the researcher manipulates an independent variable and measures its effects, if any, on a dependent variable. Write down the independent variable and dependent variable in this experiment.

> Independent variable: _____
>
> Dependent variable: _____

There are a number of experimental designs. The two most common are the independent groups or repeated measures designs. Which was used in this study? To understand this, it is useful to consider what is being compared. If you are comparing the results of two different groups of people (one group in each condition) the method is an independent group design. If you are comparing the results of one group of people in two different conditions, the design is a repeated measure design.

> The design used in this study was:
>
> _____

Hint

To work out your IV, think about what happened to you between making your first estimate (condition 1) and making your second estimate (condition 2), for example group discussion and group estimate.

Think about it

What particular extraneous variables need to be addressed when these two different designs are used?

Write a suitable hypothesis for the study you have just done. The experimental hypothesis predicts a difference between the conditions. You will need to decide whether your experimental hypothesis should be directional or non-directional. Directional hypotheses are chosen when there is sufficient research to point to the outcome of the study. A non-directional hypothesis is used when you do not know the likely influence of the independent variable.

Write your hypotheses here.

_____

_____

_____

_____

> **Hint**
>
> Do you think the estimates will move towards the one that came from the group discussion or away from it? If you have no idea which way they will go from previous research findings, that would need a non-directional hypothesis.

Justify your choice of a directional or non-directional hypothesis here.

I have chosen a _____ *hypothesis because* _____

_____

_____

_____

Step 2 *The ethical issues of the study*

Ethical issues guide practical choices and decisions at all stages of the research process. Think about the ethical issues involved in this piece of research.

- An important principle of research is to enable participants to give their fully informed consent to take part. You should have had an information sheet that told you what was involved in the study, what you would be asked to do and roughly how long it would take. This information should have included a consent form that you were asked to sign. The consent form should have made it clear that you were free to withdraw at any time.

- Debriefing information should have been given (usually in written form with verbal support) at the end of the study. This should have explained what the experiment was about and the findings that were expected and it should have asked whether participants had any questions.

Step 3 *The sample used in the study*

There are three types of sample you are required to know about:

- a random sample
- an opportunity sample
- a self-selected (volunteer) sample.

> **Look it up ...**
>
> Remind yourself about the advantages and disadvantages of each of these sampling methods by looking in your AS Student Book or another resource.

In this study, your class acted as a group of participants. You were all asked to participate because you were in the class.

> *Which sample method does this represent?*
>
> _____

Step 4 **The stimulus materials and data sheets used in the study**

Review the materials used in the study. Firstly, look at the information sheet and consent form. The information sheet only gives a vague description of what you will do later in this study. However, it does not mention that the study is about informational conformity. This does not really allow you to give fully informed consent.

> *Why did your teacher or tutor not give all of the information needed for fully informed consent for this particular practical?*
>
> _____
>
> _____
>
> _____
>
> _____

The standard instructions for the experiment should be clear and describe exactly what to do.

The debriefing sheet should give the full information and the hypothesis of the study because it was not given in the information sheet (you were not told it was a study of conformity).

Analysing your data

Step 5 *Descriptive analysis of your results*

You should have two sets of individual scores and a group estimate from the investigation. The two sets of individual scores are the original estimates and the estimates after the group discussion. These are the two sets of scores you will be comparing.

Typically you would compare two sets of scores by comparing a measure of central tendency. Such measures are not useful here because you want to see whether individuals have moved their estimates closer to the group estimate. Some participants may have moved their estimates up and some may have moved them down, so the average figure may not change. The simplest way of recording

---

Think about controls

Control is an important principle of research design. One important element of control is to have standardised stimulus materials and instructions.

Think about validity

The type of conformity studied here only works if participants do not think they know the answer. Was estimating the number of beans in a jar an ambiguous task (i.e. the exact answer was not knowable or definite)?

Ethical issues

Informed consent was not given at the beginning of the study. Apart from more detailed information, what other details could be emphasised in the debriefing sheet?

change in the study is to use nominal data. That is, for each participant, record 'yes' if they moved closer to the group estimate or 'no' if they stayed the same/moved away from the group score in a table like the one below.

Participant	Original individual estimate	Group estimate	Revised individual estimate	Moved closer to group?
1	515	420	450	Yes
2	310	420	390	Yes
3	400	420	400	No

Calculate the number of yes and no answers as a percentage of the total number of participants.

Measures of dispersion might be a useful tool to show any changes in the estimates. If most participants are moving their extreme low and high scores towards a group figure, you might expect the dispersion of scores to be smaller in the second set of scores. You could use one (or more) of these three measures:

- Range – this might show a difference between the first and second set of estimates, but it might be distorted if there is still the odd extreme high and low score in the second set.
- Inter-quartile range – this removes the extremes and might give a better representation of any changes in the two sets of scores.
- Standard deviation – this gives a good indication of the dispersion of scores because it takes into account the deviation of every individual score from the mean.

Step 6 *Displaying your data in tables and graphs*

Draw up a table to show the percentages of participants who did and did not change their estimate after the group discussion. Remember that tables should be fully labelled and clear. It should be obvious to someone reading the table what your results were. You will need a separate table to show the measures of dispersion for the two conditions.

Another way of showing patterns of data is to use graphs. As graphs are visual representations of the patterns in data, they should be easy to understand and, for many people, easier to recall as they read the conclusion and discussion. There are many types of graphs including:

- histograms
- bar charts
- scattergrams.

Which type of graph is appropriate to show the percentages of participants who did and did not change their estimate?

_____

> **Hint**
>
> The specification does not require you to know the inter-quartile range, but it could be useful. It is like finding the range of the middle 50 per cent of the scores. You put the sets of estimates in value order (as when finding the median) and remove the top quarter and bottom quarter of the results. The difference between the highest and the lowest estimate is the IQR or inter-quartile range. Comparing these, do they converge towards the median (give a lower IQR and become less spread out)?

Critical discussion

Theory

- Did your findings support the hypothesis that most participants would change their estimates to be closer to the group estimate?
- Do you think that participants were truly influenced by the group discussion or were they responding to demand characteristics in the experiment?

Methodology

- Was estimating the number of beans a useful way of measuring conformity or could it have been improved? (Was it ambiguous enough?)
- Did the study have ecological validity?
- Were the standardised instructions clear?
- Were the 'individual' estimates individual or did classmates discuss the answer in small groups? (Were there whispered conversations?)
- Can you suggest any ways the practical could be improved?

Ethics

- Did the study throw up any unseen ethical issues with your class?
- How did you feel about taking part?
- What have you learned about research with people?

> **Think about validity**
>
> Do you think that you and your classmates behaved normally in this study? If you think that similar results could have been obtained in a different, maybe real-life, situation then the study has ecological validity. However, if the results were the product of being in a class and having instructions from a teacher then the study probably does not have ecological validity.

References

Jenness, A. (1932) The role of discussion in changing opinion regarding matter of fact. *Journal of Abnormal and Social Psychology*, **27**, 279–96.

Sherif, M. (1936) *The Psychology of Social Norms*. New York: Harper & Row.

Social psychology

8   Locus of control

> **Learning outcomes in this practical**
> - A1, A2, A4, A6, B1, B2, B4, B5, B6, B7, B8, B10, C2, C3, C5, C7

> **Hint**
>
> Check these learning outcomes against the list on pages iv–v.

Student practical

In this practical you are going to examine the possible link between conformity and a characteristic known as locus of control. This exercise will work best if you perform it in pairs and pool your data for analysis.

Background

We are influenced by other people in many different ways. One of these social influences is conformity. When we conform with others, we adopt similar behaviours, beliefs or attitudes.

A glance around your classmates will remind you how people differ in the tendency to conform with social rules. One type of conformity is to different styles of dress. If you are in a college where you are able to wear your own clothes, look at how people are dressed. Some people are strongly conformist, choosing to blend in with the crowd, whereas others appear to enjoy standing out and breaking the rules. On a school non-uniform day, it is quite common to find that almost everyone has appeared to have dressed virtually identically. What leads to these differences in the tendency to conform and what makes some people resist pressures to follow the crowd?

One explanation of conformity was put forward by Julian Rotter in 1966. Rotter argued that conformity is related to a characteristic that he called 'locus of control'. Locus of control refers to an individual's sense of personal control over events in their life and is measured on a scale. At one end of the scale there are people with an internal locus of control (ILC). They largely believe that things that happen to them are due to the actions and choices they make. It has been suggested that 'internals' are less easily influenced and therefore less likely to conform to others. In contrast, individuals with an external locus of control (ELC) tend to believe that they cannot control things that happen to them and that things occur due to fate or luck, for example. 'Externals' are thought to be more likely to conform with others and less likely to stand out from the crowd. This practical investigates the possible link between conformity and locus of control.

> **Look it up ...**
>
> You can find Rotter's locus of control scale in the Appendix on pages 65–6. You might want to try it yourself before you proceed with this practical.

Background studies

In the 1970s and 1980s there was considerable interest in conformity and locus of control. However, research studies produced different findings, as you can see from the three summaries included below.

Singh (1984) studied male students who were asked to complete a locus of control scale. Twenty students with the highest scores and 20 with the lowest scores were selected and divided into two groups of internals and externals. The students then took part in Asch-style experiments in groups of five made up wholly of internals or wholly of externals.

Singh found that the groups of externals were more likely to conform to each other's views. They reached an agreement more rapidly than the internals.

Kulreshtha and Kashyap (2004) investigated conformity to fashion trends in teenage girls. A sample of 200 girls aged 13–18 completed a clothing conformity scale that measured how much they followed fashion trends. They also completed a modified version of Rotter's LC scale. The researchers found that girls with an external LC were more likely to conform to fashion trends than those with an internal LC.

However, Williams and Warchal (1981) studied 30 students, giving them conformity tasks similar to Asch's line experiment. Each student was then asked to complete a locus of control questionnaire (scale). Williams and Warchal found no relationship between conformity and locus of control.

Method

Step 1 *The design of the study: variables and hypotheses*

The first step of the research process is to identify a topic of interest and to choose a suitable method to investigate it. In this practical, you are going to examine the possible relationship between conformity to fashion trends and locus of control in a similar way to Kulreshtha and Kashyap. The method you will use is correlation.

In a correlation, the researcher measures two co-variables and examines them to see whether a relationship exists between them. Write these in the spaces below.

> *Variable 1:* _____
>
> *Variable 2:* _____

An important part of this practical will be thinking about how to operationalise (define and measure) these variables. Different ways of doing this are considered in Step 4.

Write a suitable hypothesis for the study. The experimental hypothesis predicts a relationship between the conditions. You will need to decide whether your experimental hypothesis should be directional or non-directional. Remember that non-directional hypotheses are chosen when there is little previous research, or studies have produced inconsistent or contradictory findings.

Write your hypothesis here.

Justify your choice of a directional or non-directional hypothesis here.

I have chosen a _____ *hypothesis because* _____

Step 2 *Consider ethical issues*

Ethical issues guide practical choices and decisions at all stages of the research process. Think about the ethical issues involved in this piece of research. You are going to study a group of people who will be asked about their behaviour/ tendency to conform to fashion trends. They will also be asked to complete a questionnaire measuring their locus of control.

- An important principle of research is to enable participants to give their informed consent to take part, knowing what they will be letting themselves in for. You will need to ensure that you **inform your participants that the study involves questions about their attitudes to fashion and aspects of their personality** (LC). You may not want to tell them precisely what your hypothesis is at the start to avoid the possibility of demand characteristics. Withholding details of this nature is acceptable as long as you fully debrief your participants at the end of the study. You should explain to your participants roughly how long the procedures will take. This information should be included in a consent form that you ask the participants to sign before they agree to take part. The consent form should make it clear to the participants that they are free to withdraw from the study at any time.

- Another important ethical principle is the need for confidentiality. You should **ensure that your participants' results/scores are recorded using a method that does not allow them to be identified.** Ensure that the two measurements for each participant can be paired. Initials and numbers are generally a good way of achieving this.

■ Your participants should be given debriefing information after they have taken part in the data collection. You should provide them with a standard debriefing sheet at the end of the study. This should tell them exactly what the study was about and what you expected to find. You should also ask whether they have questions about the study. Remember that the purpose of debriefing is to ensure that your participants go away feeling as good as when they started.

Step 3 *Sampling*

You will need to select a sample of people to take part in your study. You should ensure that your participants are aged between 16 and 19. In order to have sufficient data to analyse, you will need between 12 and 20 participants. The original study used females only and you may want to think about whether to carry out your study using females, males or both. If you choose to use males *and* females, you will need to devise your fashion conformity scale so that it is suitable for both sexes.

You are required to know about three types of sample:

■ a random sample

■ an opportunity sample

■ a self-selected (volunteer) sample.

Think about the advantages and disadvantages of each of these types of sample and decide which method you intend to use. Record this below.

> **Look it up ...**
>
> You might want to remind yourself about the advantages and disadvantages of each of these sampling methods.

Chosen sampling method and reasons for choice:

_____

_____

_____

Step 4 *Designing your measuring scales, standardised instructions and data record sheets*

An important task in a correlational study is deciding how the variables are going to be measured. This has been made easy for you in relation to locus of control where you should use Rotter's LC scale. You can find an adapted version of the LC scale in the Appendix on pages 65–6. The scale consists of 29 questions, each of which requires respondents to choose either answer a or answer b.

You will find a scoring system for the LC scale on page 66. The maximum score is 23 and scores from around 16 and above indicate an external locus of control. The minimum score is 0 and scores from 0 to 8 indicate an internal locus of control.

As you can see from the scoring system, six questions are discounted and do not receive a score. Have a look at these and think why they have been included in the questionnaire.

Why are unscored items included in the questionnaire?

_____

_____

_____

_____

How are you going to measure conformity to fashion trends? Kulreshtha and Kashyap measured this by devising a clothing conformity scale. There are various methods of measuring clothing conformity. If ethical principles allowed, you could surreptitiously observe your classmates for several days to see what they wear. However, in this practical you should **devise a clothing conformity questionnaire**. This should have around 10 closed questions with four tick-box answers similar to the following examples:

- I have bought an item of clothing that I have seen in a fashion magazine (often, sometimes, rarely, never)
- I have bought an item of clothing because two or three of my friends had bought it (often, sometimes, rarely, never)

Using four tick-box responses will make it easy for you to calculate a score for your questionnaire. You should **award three marks for often, two for sometimes, one for rarely and zero for never**. Assuming there are 10 questions, this will give a maximum score of 30 and a minimum score of 0. **When you have designed your conformity scale, print it on a single A4 sheet of paper.**

Design a set of standardised instructions for your participants. These should state clearly what you expect them to do. You can print these on the top of the conformity questionnaire if you want.

Finally, you should **prepare a data sheet on which to record your results.** It should allow you to record the initials of each participant and their scores for both measures.

> **Hint**
>
> If you wish, you can refer to current fashionable items in your questionnaire.

> **Look it up …**
>
> You may recall that questionnaires use two types of question – closed and open. Closed questions with pre-set answers make it easier to calculate a score and compare people, both of which are important here.

Participant initials	Conformity score	LC score
L.H.	24	21
P.J.	26	13
K.L.	17	16

Step 5 *Piloting*

Now try out your materials and standardised instructions with a couple of people to see whether they work. You will need to decide the order in which you ask your participants to complete the two tasks. Think about the pros and cons of doing the LC scale or the conformity test first. Record your decision and a brief reason for it here.

Decision and reason for it:

_____

_____

_____

_____

_____

Remember that your pilot study is an important part of the research process, enabling you to test your materials and check that everything works well. You may find that your standardised instructions need altering, or some of your questions need rephrasing if people do not understand them.

Record any changes that you make to your methods and materials as a result of your pilot study.

_____

_____

_____

_____

_____

When you are satisfied that everything works correctly, you can go ahead and collect your data.

Analysing your data

Step 6 *Display your data using a suitable graph*

Your data sheet should have two sets of scores for each participant. One will be their conformity to fashion score and the other will be their locus of control score. **Plot these scores on a scattergram.** This is the most suitable graph for a correlational study as it shows how the two variables relate to each other. It

Think about it

If you tried your clothing conformity questionnaire out on someone you thought of as being very concerned about following fashion and someone you thought was not, would you be assessing validity or reliability?

Hint

Remember that your pilot study should also stick to the ethical principles covered above.

will help you to see whether there is a relationship between the participants' conformity score and their LC score.

In a scattergram, each axis relates to a variable. Although, technically speaking, it does not matter which variable you put on which axis, in this example you should put the conformity scores on the horizontal (x) axis and the locus of control score on the vertical (y) axis. Ensure that each axis starts at the lowest possible score and ends at the highest possible score. Remember to give your scattergram a title and to label both axes appropriately. Your graph can be drawn on graph paper or presented using a spreadsheet program, such as Excel.

Scattergram of LC scores and conformity scores

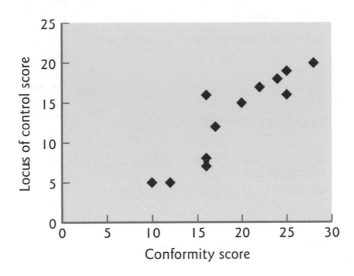

Look at your scattergram. **Describe the pattern shown by your data** using the terms 'positive correlation' or 'negative correlation' and 'weak', 'moderate' or 'strong'. The above example (based on fabricated data) shows a strong positive correlation. You can tell it is positive as high scores on conformity are matched with high scores on LC. It is a strong correlation as it shows a clear 'trend' with the points falling in a line. You could also describe your correlation by estimating the correlation coefficient. In the above example, the correlation coefficient would be between +0.8 and +0.9.

Describe your own correlation here.

_____

_____

_____

_____

Critical discussion

Theory

■ Did your findings support Kulreshtha and Kashyap or contradict them?

■ If you found no relationship, can you think of reasons why this might be?

■ Can you comment on the reliability, validity or conformity of the scale?

Methodology

■ What order did you use to present your two scales? Did this work and how could it have been improved?

■ Was your measuring scale a useful way of measuring conformity to fashion?

■ Did you include useful questions/items or could your conformity scale have been improved?

■ Did your study have ecological validity?

■ Were your standardised instructions clear?

■ Can you suggest any ways the practical could be improved?

Ethics

■ Did your study throw up any unseen ethical issues?

■ How did people feel about taking part?

■ What have you learned about research with people?

Think about validity

You could have carried out this study by observing people and rating them for conformity to fashion rather than asking them to complete your scale. How do you think this would have influenced the data and the outcome of the study? Would it have provided a better measurement of conformity than the self-report method used?

References

Kulreshtha, U. and Kashyap, R. (2004) Clothing conformity in adolescents. *Journal of Indian Academy of Applied Psychology*, **30**(1–2), 21–7.

Rotter, J.B. (1966) Generalized expectations for internal versus external control of reinforcement. *Psychological Monographs*, **80**, whole no. 609.

Singh, R.P. (1984) Experimental verification of locus of control as related to conformity behaviour. *Psychological Studies*, **29**(1), 64–7.

Williams, J. and Warchal, J. (1981) Relationship between assertiveness, internal-external locus of control and overt conformity. *Journal of Psychology – Interdisciplinary and Applied*, **109**(1), 93–6.

Glossary

Bar chart: a method of representing data from a discrete variable on a graph. Bar height corresponds to individual scores or frequency.

Case study: detailed information that is gathered about an individual or group of people to create a case history.

Closed questions: questions in which the participant chooses their response from a limited number of fixed answers.

Coding: Processing qualitative data by counting instances (of words themes or concepts) that correspond to particular categories.

Confidentiality: the ethical principle that participants have the right to expect that data regarding their identity or scores, etc. should not be disclosed to those outside the research setting.

Consent form: a form that is used before a piece of research takes place. The participant signs it to show they agree to take part.

Content analysis: a way of studying qualitative data that involves setting up categories and coding the data into them and so counting how many times they occur. It can be used in a variety of formats: text, images or spoken word or behaviours can all be coded.

Controlled observation: observation in which the researcher controls certain variables, often in a laboratory setting.

Data record sheet: a sheet on which scores are recorded.

Debriefing sheet: a sheet that is given to participants, usually supported verbally after they have taken part in a research study. It provides detailed information about the aims of the study and thanks them for participating.

Demand characteristics: cues in the environment that help the participant work out what the research hypothesis is. This can lead to social desirability effects where the participant behaves in a way that the hypothesis will be supported or the 'screw you' effect where the participant purposefully disrupts the research.

Dependent variable (DV): the variable that is affected by changes in the independent variable (IV).

Descriptive statistics: techniques used to summarise data.

Descriptive survey: a survey that aims to describe the behaviour of respondents.

Event sampling: a method used in observational studies where behaviours are recorded each time they occur.

Experiment: a research investigation in which one specific variable is manipulated to observe its effect, if any, on another specific variable, while keeping all other variables constant. In a true experiment, participants are randomly allocated to conditions or take part in all conditions.

Experimental hypothesis: a predictive statement used in the context of an experiment.

Extraneous variables: in experiments anything other than the IV that affects the DV. Consideration and steps should be taken to stop them affecting the results.

Field experiment: an experiment that takes place in a natural environment: the independent variable is manipulated.

Histogram: a visual representation of continuous data as a graph with adjacent rectangles. The area of the rectangles represents the frequency. Usually have equal class widths so frequency is proportional height.

Hypothesis: a precise, testable statement about the expected outcome of an investigation.

Independent measures (or independent groups) design: participants take part in only one of the conditions.

Independent variable (IV): the variable that the researcher manipulates and which is assumed to have a direct effect on the dependent variable.

Institutionalisation: refers to the behaviour patterns of children who have been raised in institutions such as orphanages or children's homes. In institutions, children may have relationships with a variety of staff. However, they may not have a one-to-one attachment in the same way as a child raised in a family.

Investigator (or researcher) effects: the researcher influencing the result of an experiment towards what they think the research outcome should be perhaps at an unconscious level.

Matched participant (or matched pairs) design: participants are paired up with regard to variables such age, intelligence or personality traits and then one of each pair is randomly allocated to one or other of the conditions.

Mean: the statistical average, calculated by adding up all the scores in a set of data and then dividing by the number of scores.

Median: the median is a central value of a data set, and is calculated by first putting the data in order and then finding the middle score. If there is an even number of scores, you should add the two middle scores together and divide by two.

Mode: the mode is the most frequently occurring score and is calculated by a frequency count – quite simply, analyse your data and see which score occurs the most frequently.

Naturalistic observation: this takes place when a researcher records naturally occurring behaviours without intervening.

Non-verbal behaviour: often known as non-verbal communication, it includes behaviours such as gestures and facial expressions.

Open question: a question that participants answer using their own words.

Operationalising: the process of devising a way of measuring a variable.

Opportunity sample: a sample of people selected because they are readily available and convenient for the researcher to study, such as family or friends.

Personality: consistent features of an individual that lead them to behave in a particular way.

Privation: literally the lack of something. Emotional privation is the lack of attachment or love in a child who has been unable to form an attachment. Physical privation refers to the lack of basic physical needs such as food or shelter.

Qualitative data: non-numerical data often in the form of words taken from interviews.

Questionnaire: a written set of questions that can be given to a large number of people.

Random sample: a sample in which every member of the target population has an equal chance of being selected.

Range: the difference between the highest and lowest score in a set of data.

Reliability: measuring something consistently. For instance, someone else should get the same result if measuring the same thing.

Repeated measures design: participants take part in all conditions.

Research questions: an open question often used in qualitative research, which does not make a prediction.

Retrospective informed consent: asking participants for their consent after they have taken part in a study.

Scattergram: a graphical technique that gives a picture of the relationship between two variables.

Self-selected (volunteer) sampling: where subjects volunteer themselves for a study after seeing an advert.

Sequential process: the idea that attitude change takes place in a series of stages.

Standardised instructions: a set of instructions that are given in an identical form to all participants.

Structured interview: an interview in which all participants are asked the same questions in the same order.

Subjective: something that can be interpreted by individuals in different ways.

Survey: a large-scale research method that uses questionnaires to collect the views of a large sample of people.

Thematic analysis: a method of analysing qualitative data by looking for themes.

Type A personality: a behaviour pattern associated with high stress levels. Characteristics include time pressure, hostility and competitiveness.

Unstructured observation: the researcher uses direct observation to record behaviours as they occur; there is no predetermined plan about what particular behaviours will be observed.

Validity: actually measuring what is claimed to be being measured.

Appendix

BPS Guidelines for research with human participants

The British Psychological Society code of ethics, *Ethical Principles for Conducting Research with Human Participants*, covers nine different aspects of ethics that relate to research with human participants:

- Consent: participants should give informed consent.
- Deception: participants should not be misled.
- Debriefing: following the investigation, the study should be discussed with participants.
- Withdrawal from investigation: participants should feel free to leave the investigation at any time.
- Confidentiality: participants have the right to confidentiality.
- Protection of participants: this includes both physical and psychological harm.
- Observational research: the privacy of participants needs to be respected.
- Giving advice: psychologists should only give advice for which they are qualified.
- Colleagues: psychologists have a duty to make sure all research is ethical, and this includes colleagues.

Check the BPS website for the most up-to-date *Ethical Principles for Conducting Research with Human Participants* (see the link to the 'Code of Conduct and Ethical Guidelines' on 'The Society' page).

Sample consent form

Consent form
Please tick the box by each statement if you agree with it.
I have read the information sheet and understand what I will will be asked to do. ☐
I have been given time to consider whether I wish to participate and to ask any questions I have about the study. ☐
I understand I have the right to withdraw at any point. ☐
I understand that I have the right to withdraw my data. ☐
I consent to participate in the study ☐
Signed _____

Example information sheet

Information about the study

What will I be asked to do?
There will be two parts to the study. In the first part, you will be asked to look at a number of female faces. In the second part, you will be shown more faces and be asked to recognise the original faces. In the second part of the study, the faces will either be presented upright or inverted.

How long will it take?
The two stages of the study will take approximately 15 minutes.

Can I change my mind?
Yes, you have the right to withdraw at any stage of the study. You can also withhold your data by not submitting your response sheet. The response sheets are numbered. Please make a note of your number and quote it if you wish to withdraw your data after the study (up to one week after the study).

What will happen to my results?
Your response sheets will be used to collate data for the experiment. You will not be asked to identify yourself on the response sheets and all data will therefore be anonymous. All data will be completely confidential. Your response sheet will be kept by the researcher for one week while the data is being collated and then will be sent for secure confidential disposal.

Are there any benefits for me?
Yes, you will gain experience of participating in a psychology study.

Are there any disadvantages for me?
We do not anticipate any disadvantages to you. All efforts have been made to eliminate the risk of any harm to you. If you do have any concerns that you wish to discuss, please contact the head of Psychology.

Case study scenarios (for use in Chapter 4)

Case study 1: Raluca

Background information

Raluca spent around four months in a very deprived Romanian orphanage before she was adopted at the age of nine months by Sue and David. Sue and David have no other children. Sue gave up her job as a social worker to look after Raluca until she started school. Raluca is now six years old.

Sue's story: When we adopted Raluca, she was slightly developmentally delayed and was unable to sit up at nine months. Raluca made rapid progress after adoption. She reached the average height and weight for a child of her age by the time she was one and rapidly caught up with lots of her milestones. She walked at 15 months (which is a bit later than usual) and said her first words at around 18 months.

In those pre-school years, I really devoted my whole time to Raluca and she was never left with a babysitter or childminder as I wanted her to attach to me. I think having Raluca has made me much more patient and understanding than I used to be. From being placid and undemanding, Raluca became very demanding indeed. When she was about 18 months and just walking, she followed me everywhere, even into the bathroom! I can remember one day when I wanted to use the loo in peace, and closed the door and Raluca lay on the floor and I could see her hair coming under the door – a bit like a horror film! I am much less likely to worry about inessential things since I became Raluca's mum.

We started going to playgroup when Raluca was two but I always stayed with Raluca, rather than leaving her for the morning. Initially she was very wary of the other children – hung back, would not play at the sand tray if anyone else was there. She is a bit better now but she stays very close to the teacher and the playground supervisors and does not have that much confidence to play with other children. There is still quite a long way to go there I think.

David's story: I agree with Sue that adopting Raluca was the best thing we have done. When we adopted Raluca, she was a very small baby indeed, weighing only 6.2 kg. Raluca had poor physical health – she had recurrent stomach upsets and had not started on solid food. She still has some health problems including a very sensitive stomach and recurrent eczema and she has been very slow to toilet train. When she started school at four-and-a-half years, she was still not reliably dry in the day and would often wet the bed at night. Raluca developed a very close bond with Sue – perhaps because she was with her all day – but when I got home from work, Raluca would demand my attention continually. She was very difficult to put to bed at night and if Sue and I left her before she went to sleep, she would scream and soon learned to escape from her cot. We developed a system of one or other of us sitting with Raluca until she was asleep – which may not have been ideal but it was less wearing than continually going back up the stairs. I found this exhausting – especially as Raluca would wake in the night two or three times – but this improved when she started school. I think it tired her out! Raluca is a lovely little girl – she is bright and interested in everything. I am so proud that she has developed as well as this. But I do think that it would be difficult to adopt another child as Raluca still needs all of our attention.

Case study 2: Ivan

Background information

Ivan was adopted at the age of 19 months by Safi and Peter. They have two older children, Katy (14) and Joshua (12) but were able to adopt Ivan as policies are less strict for older babies. Ivan had been in the orphanage for about 15 months when he was adopted and he showed signs of developmental delay. He has been looked after by Peter in the daytime. Ivan is now five years old and has recently started full-time mainstream school.

Peter's story: One of the real benefits of having Ivan has been the impact on our other two children. Before we adopted Ivan, they used to squabble and fight quite a lot more, but both are now much less selfish and more mature. Katy is talking about training as a children's nurse when she leaves school.

Because Safi earns more money, we decided that I should stay at home and look after Ivan until he started school. We did not want to leave him with a childminder although we had done this with Katy and Josh. Ivan showed quite a lot of stereotyped behaviours when he was young. He used to rock backwards and forwards – I think it was one of few things he could do in the cot. He has almost dropped it now, but sometimes if things get stressful at nursery or school, he will start rocking. If he does it at home, we ignore it or distract him with a toy and he soon stops. He is also pretty easy to distract with food – but we do keep an eye on that as Ivan does not know when to stop eating and can be pretty greedy. Last Christmas, he ate until he was sick three or four times.

Ivan gets on very well with other children. He is quite popular at school and is an outgoing little boy. He has a best friend (Sam from next door) who is in the same school class. I think having two older siblings helped Ivan to develop socially quite quickly after his early start.

Safi's story: After we had seen the programmes about Romanian orphanages, we just had to help out and Ivan was the child who really tugged at our hearts when we visited. At the time of adoption, Ivan was a very small baby and he showed serious signs of malnutrition. He had poor physical health, suffering from recurrent stomach upsets and sleep terrors and still does not sleep the night through even though he is almost five. Ivan showed severe signs of developmental delay. He was unable to walk as he had been confined to a cot and had built up no muscles. He had to have physiotherapy for the first six months and started walking when he was just two years old. He could not say any words at 19 months and started talking properly when he was three years old. I think this was because Josh and Katy spent so much time talking to him. Ivan has continued to have quite a lot of health problems and has difficulties with eating a normal diet. He will also over-eat until he is sick, especially at birthday parties, if we do not keep an eye on him.

Negative Event Scale (for use in Chapter 6)

You are asked to think about the negative events (hassles) that you have *experienced in the last month*.

Below are a list of items that can be negative events. For each item, consider first if the event occurred *during the last month* and then how **hassled** you felt.

Please remember that it is important that you:

> * circle one number for *each item even if there was no hassle*
> * consider each item with only *the last month in mind*.

How much of a <u>hassle</u> was this negative event?

0 = Did not occur
1 = Event occurred but there was no hassle
2 = Event occurred and a little of a hassle
3 = Event occurred and somewhat of a hassle
4 = Event occurred and a lot of a hassle
5 = Event occurred and an extreme hassle

In the last month

Problems with friends

1	Negative feedback from your friend/s	0	1	2	3	4	5
2	Negative communication with friend/s	0	1	2	3	4	5
3	Conflict with a friend/s	0	1	2	3	4	5
4	Disagreement (including arguments) with a friend/s	0	1	2	3	4	5

Problems with your spouse/partner (boy/girl friend)

5	Negative communication with your spouse/partner (boy/girl friend)	0	1	2	3	4	5
6	Conflict with spouse/partner (boy/girl friend)	0	1	2	3	4	5
7	Disagreement (including arguments) with spouse/partner (boy/girl friend)	0	1	2	3	4	5
8	Rejection by your spouse/partner (boy/girl friend)	0	1	2	3	4	5
9	Your spouse/partner (boy/girl friend) let you down	0	1	2	3	4	5

Work

10	The nature of your job/work (if employed)	0	1	2	3	4	5
11	Your workload	0	1	2	3	4	5
12	Meeting deadlines or goals on the job	0	1	2	3	4	5
13	Use of your skills at work	0	1	2	3	4	5

Money

14	Not enough money for necessities (e.g. food, clothing, housing, healthcare, taxes, insurance, etc.)	0	1	2	3	4	5
15	Not enough money for education	0	1	2	3	4	5
16	Not enough money for emergencies	0	1	2	3	4	5
17	Not enough money for extras (e.g. entertainment, recreation, vacations, etc.)	0	1	2	3	4	5

Problems with children

18	Negative communication with your child(ren)	0	1	2	3	4	5
19	Conflict with your child(ren)	0	1	2	3	4	5
20	Disagreement (including arguments) with your child(ren)	0	1	2	3	4	5

Course

21	Your study load	0	1	2	3	4	5
22	Study/course deadlines	0	1	2	3	4	5
23	Time pressures	0	1	2	3	4	5
24	Problems getting assignments/essays finished	0	1	2	3	4	5

Problems with teachers/lecturers

25	Negative communication with teacher/s, lecturer/s	0	1	2	3	4	5
26	Negative feedback from teacher/s, lecturer/s	0	1	2	3	4	5
27	Conflict with teacher/s, lecturer/s	0	1	2	3	4	5
28	Disagreement (including arguments) with your teacher/s, lecturer/s	0	1	2	3	4	5

Problems with parents or parents-in-law

29	Negative communication with your parents or parents-in-law	0	1	2	3	4	5
30	Conflict with your parents or parents-in-law	0	1	2	3	4	5
31	Disagreement (including arguments) with parents or parents-in-law	0	1	2	3	4	5
32	Negative feedback from your parents or parents-in-law	0	1	2	3	4	5

Problems with other students

33	Negative communication with other student/s	0	1	2	3	4	5
34	Conflict with other student/s	0	1	2	3	4	5
35	Disagreement (including arguments) with other student/s	0	1	2	3	4	5
36	Doing things with other student/s	0	1	2	3	4	5

Problems with relative/s

37	Conflict with other relative	0	1	2	3	4	5
38	Disagreement (including arguments) with other relative	0	1	2	3	4	5
39	Negative feedback from other relative	0	1	2	3	4	5
40	Doing things with other relative	0	1	2	3	4	5

Health problems

41	Your health	0	1	2	3	4	5
42	Your physical abilities	0	1	2	3	4	5
43	Your medical care	0	1	2	3	4	5
44	Getting sick (e.g. flu, colds)	0	1	2	3	4	5

Problems with your work supervisor/employer

45	Negative feedback from your supervisor/employer	0	1	2	3	4	5
46	Negative communication with your supervisor/employer	0	1	2	3	4	5
47	Conflict with your supervisor/employer	0	1	2	3	4	5
48	Disagreement (including arguments) with your supervisor/employer	0	1	2	3	4	5

Hassles getting a job

49	Finding a job (e.g. interviews, placements)	0	1	2	3	4	5
50	Finding work	0	1	2	3	4	5
51	Problems with finding a job	0	1	2	3	4	5
52	Employment problems (e.g. finding, losing a job)	0	1	2	3	4	5

Academic limitations

53	Not getting the marks (results) you expected	0	1	2	3	4	5
54	Your academic ability not as good as you thought	0	1	2	3	4	5
55	Not understanding some subjects	0	1	2	3	4	5

Course interest

56	Course not relevant to your future career	0	1	2	3	4	5
57	Your course is boring	0	1	2	3	4	5

Rotter's locus of control scale (for use in Chapter 8)

For each pair of statements, choose the one that you believe to be the most accurate.

1a Children get into trouble because their patents punish them too much.
1b The trouble with most children nowadays is that their parents are too easy with them.

2a Many of the unhappy things in people's lives are partly due to bad luck.
2b People's misfortunes result from the mistakes they make.

3a One of the major reasons why we have wars is because people don't take enough interest in politics.
3b There will always be wars, no matter how hard people try to prevent them.

4a In the long run people get the respect they deserve in this world.
4b Unfortunately, an individual's worth often passes unrecognised no matter how hard s/he tries.

5a The idea that teachers are unfair to students is nonsense.
5b Most students don't realise the extent to which their grades are influenced by accidental happenings.

6a Without the right breaks, one cannot be an effective leader.
6b Capable people who fail to become leaders have not taken advantage of their opportunities.

7a No matter how hard you try, some people just don't like you.
7b People who can't get others to like them don't understand how to get along with others.

8a Heredity plays the major role in determining one's personality.
8b It is one's experiences in life which determine what they're like.

9a I have often found that what is going to happen, will happen.
9b Trusting fate has never turned out as well for me as making a decision to take a definite course of action.

10a In the case of the well-prepared student there is rarely, if ever, such a thing as an unfair test.
10b Many times, exam questions tend to be so unrelated to course work that studying is really useless.

11a Becoming a success is a matter of hard work, luck has little or nothing to do with it.
11b Getting a good job depends mainly on being in the right place at the right time.

12a The average citizen can have an influence in government decisions.
12b This world is run by the few people in power, and there is not much the little guy can do about it.

13a When I make plans, I am almost certain that I can make them work.
13b It is not always wise to plan too far ahead because many things turn out to be a matter of good or bad fortune anyhow.

14a There are certain people who are just no good.
14b There is some good in everybody.

15a In my case getting what I want has little or nothing to do with luck.
15b Many times we might just as well decide what to do by flipping a coin.

16a Who gets to be the boss often depends on who was lucky enough to be in the right place first.
16b Getting people to do the right thing depends upon ability – luck has little or nothing to do with it.

17a As far as world affairs are concerned, most of us are the victims of forces we can neither understand nor control.

17b By taking an active part in political and social affairs the people can control world events.

18a Most people don't realise the extent to which their lives are controlled by accidental happenings.

18b There really is no such thing as 'luck'.

19a One should always be willing to admit mistakes.

19b It is usually best to cover up one's mistakes.

20a It is hard to know whether or not a person really likes you.

20b How many friends you have depends upon how nice a person you are.

21a In the long run the bad things that happen to us are balanced by the good ones.

21b Most misfortunes are the result of lack of ability, ignorance, laziness, or all three.

22a With enough effort we can wipe out political corruption.

22b It is difficult for people to have much control over the things politicians do in office.

23a Sometimes I can't understand how teachers arrive at the grades they give.

23b There is a direct connection between how hard I study and the grades I get.

24a A good leader expects people to decide for themselves what they should do.

24b A good leader makes it clear to everybody what their jobs are.

25a Many times I feel that I have little influence over the things that happen to me.

25b It is impossible for me to believe that chance or luck plays an important role in my life.

26a People are lonely because they don't try to be friendly.

26b There's not much use in trying too hard to please people, if they like you, they like you.

27a There is too much emphasis on athletics in high school.

27b Team sports are an excellent way to build character.

28a What happens to me is my own doing.

28b Sometimes I feel that I don't have enough control over the direction my life is taking.

29a Most of the time I can't understand why politicians behave the way they do.

29b In the long run the people are responsible for bad government on a national as well as on a local level.

Note: Dr Rotter has conditions for use of his scale:
■ Collect all copies of the scale from participants.
■ Do not publish the scale anywhere.
■ Use the scale for research purposes only.
■ Get assistance from someone with previous experience administering and interpreting personality scales if you have none yourself.

Score one point for each of the following:

2 a, 3 b, 4 b, 5 b, 6 a, 7 a, 9 a, 10 b, 11 b, 12 b, 13 b, 15 b, 16 a, 17 a, 18 a, 20 a, 21 a, 22 b, 23 a, 25 a, 26 b, 28 b, 29 a

A high score = External locus of control

A low score = Internal locus of control